How to Market Your Business Online And Offline

By Omar Johnson

This book is dedicated to my mother Flora Johnson. Your legacy lives on.

Make Profits Easy LLC. All Rights Reserved © 2012

Table of Contents

Introduction 7
Marketing Economics 9
Marketing Essentials 12
Creating a Marketing System That Runs On Autopilot 16
Direct Response Marketing 19
Characteristics of Direct Response Marketing 21
How to Market Your Business Offline 23
Direct Mail 24
The Different Formats of Direct Mail 25
The Letter 25
Sequential Follow Up Mailing System 26
A/B Split Testing 30
Mailing Lists 30
13 Direct Mail Secret Marketing Tactics 32
Postcards 35
Brochures 35
Self Mailers 36
Flyers 36
Catalogs 37
Dimensional Mailers 37
Newspaper Advertising 37
Remnant Advertising 39
How to Effectively Use Display Ads 39
Magazine Ads 41

Cable T.V. 42

Yellow Pages 42

Creating an effective Yellow Page Ad 43

Bandit Signs 44

Radio 45

Car Signs 46

Door Hangers 47

Coupons – ValPak Marketing 49

Outdoor Advertising 51

Bus Stop and Bench Signs 53

Neighborhood Bulletin Boards 55

Community Events 56

Neighborhood Publications 57

Partnership Marketing 58

How to Market Your Business Offline by Using Your Local Chamber of Commerce 58

How to Market Your Business Offline by Using a Referral Program 60

How to Market Your Business Offline with Strategic Alliances 62

How to Market Your Business Offline Using Networking Groups 64

How to Market Your Business Offline with Sponsorships 65

Event Marketing 66

How to Market Your Business Offline Using Workshops 67

How to Market Your Business Offline Using Contests 68

How to Market Your Business Offline Using Educational Seminars 70

How to Market Your Business Offline Using Speaking Engagements 71

How to Market Your Business Offline Using Trade Shows 73

How to Market Your Business Offline by having an Open House 74

How to Market Your Business Online 76

Social Media 76

How to Market Your Business Online Using LinkedIn 76

How to Market Your Business Online Using Twitter 78

How to Market Your Business Online Using Facebook 81

How to Market Your Business Online Using Google+ 83

How to Market Your Business Online Using Foursquare 85

How to Market Your Business Online Using Pinterest 87

How to Market Your Business Online Using YouTube 89

How to Market Your Business Online Using Groupon 91

How to Market Your Business Online Using Press Releases 93

Distributing Your Press Release to the Media 95

How to Market Your Business Online Using Ebooks 98

How to Market Your Business Online Using Email Marketing 101

How to Market Your Business Online Using Ezine Advertising 103

How to Market Your Business Online Using Blogs 105

Guest Blogging 108

How to Market Your Business Online Using Webinars 110

How to Market Your Business Online Using Articles 113

How to Market Your Business Online by Creating an Affiliate Program.. 115

How to Market Your Business Online Using Sponsored Reviews 117

How to Market Your Business Online Using Pay Per Click Advertising.... 119

How to Market Your Business Online Using Online Classified Ads 122

How to Market Your Business Online by Using Ebay 127

How to Market Your Business Online Using Amazon 130

How to Market Your Business Online Using Search Engine Marketing ... 131

How to Market Your Business Online using Online Business Directories 136

How to Market Your Business Online Using Mobile Apps 137

Creating a Mobile APP for Your Business...138

How to Market Your Business Online Using CraigsList 141

How to Market Your Business Online Using Banner Ads........................ 144

How to Market Your Business Online Using QR Codes........................... 148

Message to Market Match 149

You have to be a Disciplined Marketer... 152

Strategy and Execution are the Keys to Your Success 153

Other Books by Author 155

Introduction

A great deal of business owners and entrepreneurs find themselves in trouble because of their marketing's ineffectiveness and inefficiency. As a result of this dilemma, their businesses' are either failing or have already completely failed. It is a known fact that 95% of all business start- ups fail within the first 5 years. There are many reasons for this, such as: lack of capital, lack of resources, lack of an efficient distribution channel, not having a commercially viable product or service, stiff competition and the list goes on.

Although the list of reasons why a business has failed or is failing can go into infinity, this book will focus on correcting what I consider to be the main reason for business failings, ineffective and inefficient MARKETING. Why marketing? Simply because it is marketing that drives a business. Marketing is the fuel that produces the leads and prospects for a business. Prospects turn into customers and customers sustain a business and enables it to thrive.

So it doesn't matter what business you're in, I want you to get this through your head, the real business that you're in is the MARKETING BUSINESS. If you ignore this, you do so at your own peril. Having said that, since we essentially live in two worlds when it comes to marketing, the offline world and the online world, this book will show you how to market your business online as well as offline. Offline and online marketing go together like a horse and carriage and if done effectively can propel your business and your profits into the next stratosphere.

Marketing Goals, Tactics and Strategies

Before employing any of the marketing tactics and strategies mentioned in this book you must first decide what outcome you are looking to achieve with your marketing. The outcome that you are looking to achieve is considered to be your goal. First you would define your goal, then you would develop a strategy which is basically an idea, a conceptualization, on how that goal could be achieved. Then you would employ tactics, which are simply actions that you take to execute your strategy.

For example if your goal was to establish major search engine visibility for your business, this is a brief synopsis of how that sequence would look:

Goal:

Establish major search engine visibility

Strategy:

Assess the ranking variables that Google, Yahoo and Bing use in determining how high a website will rank for its main keywords in relation to its competition. Once those variables have been identified and assessed, they will be impacted to achieve the ultimate goal of search engine visibility for our business.

Tactics:

*Purchase an aged domain name since it is one of the variables that was identified in determining how high a website will rank in the major search engines.

*On page optimization – each page of our business website must be fully optimized (SEO) because this is another important identified variable that the major search engines use to determine which keyword(s) or keyword phrases that our website will rank for.

*Off page optimization – We have to build backlinks for our business website because this is another identified variable that determines where you rank. We will utilize the following tactics to create backlinks: Article marketing, social bookmarking, online press releases, and blog commenting.

When you take this methodical approach in formulating your marketing goals and strategy it enables you to maintain focus and achieve the results that you desire. There is no chance for you to get loss at sea because you have a map in front of you that charts your destination. All you have to do is embark and stay the course and you will inevitably reach your destination. So without further ado let's begin.

Marketing Economics

Before you begin investing money in the marketing of your products or services you should do a thorough analysis to determine whether it makes sense for you economically. Specifically, what you can do is perform a break-even analysis. A break-even analysis is used to determine how much sales volume your business needs to cover your cost of doing business. Here's the formula that you would use to determine your break-even point in units.

Break-Even In Units

$$\frac{\text{Fixed Costs}}{\text{Selling Price - Variable Costs}}$$

Here's an example so that you can understand how to apply this formula to your business. Let's say you were selling boxes of cigars retail. It costs you $25 to purchase each box wholesale (this represents your variable costs) and you retail them for $60. Your marketing budget is $7,000 for the year which represents your fixed costs. You will need to sell 200 units to break-even. Here's that calculation:

$$\frac{\$7,000}{\$60 - \$25} = \textbf{200 units or boxes of cigars}$$

Your break-even point in terms of your marketing dollars that you plan to spend may or may not be economically feasible for you. For instance, let's change the dollar amount of the marketing costs in our previous example to $50,000. Our new break-even point would now be 1,429 units.

$$\frac{\$50,000}{\$60 - \$25} = \textbf{1,429 units or boxes of cigars}$$

The questions that you have to ask yourself as a business owner are:

Can you easily surpass that break even amount to make a profit?

The whole purpose of business is to eventually make a profit not just break even. So, in this instance, if you can't see your business surpassing your break-even point by a great deal then you should either reduce your marketing costs or increase your selling price which will have the simultaneous effect of increasing the profit that you make per cigar box, and lowering the amount of units you need to sell to break-even.

Of course before you do a price increase, you have to take into account whether your vendors, distributors, or customers will buy at your new price. You also have to take into account your competition. If you're selling the same product and they are offering it at a lower price than you, then quite naturally your customers will buy from your competitors instead of you.

This is mainly because you are selling a commodity. It is a commodity because there is nothing unique about it. It's generic. So people decide to buy it or not solely based on the price. The problem with that is there are always competitors out there who are willing to sell what you are selling cheaper. They don't mind sacrificing profits. The end result? A price slashing war ensues between you and your competitors with no one really winning. Everyone that is competing with you in this price slashing manner is essentially committing a form of economic suicide.

Conversely, the way to avoid this is by selling unique products or services and if you are selling similar products or services as your competitors just differentiate and distinguish your offerings from theirs.

For example, take the company Zappos they sell shoes. Shoes are a commodity, but the way that Zappos distinguishes itself in the marketplace is by their unique offering. Their unique offering to the marketplace is, if you buy shoes from them they will ship your shoes for free and if you don't like them you can return them and the shipping is also free. To top it off, you have up to 365 days to return your shoes.

Can you afford your marketing plan?

Anyone can put together a marketing plan that defines what they would like to do in terms of marketing but the bottom line is you must always ask yourself can you afford it? Does your budget permit it? Does it tie up too much capital? You have to really do your due diligence in this department before investing your money in the marketing of your products and services. That's why I entitled this section marketing economics.

Is your pricing strategy sufficient?

Once you have determined that you have a commercially viable product or service, the prosperity of your business depends upon the effectiveness of your marketing and your pricing strategy. Your pricing strategy will determine what type of profits you will make, how sufficiently capitalized your business will be, how well you compensate your employees or staff (if you have one), your ability to acquire new customers or retain the ones that you have, and your marketing. The bottom line is, if you are working on thin margins as a result of your pricing it will adversely affect your ability to properly market your products or services to the public.

Marketing Essentials

Before we get into the nuts and bolts of how to market your business online and offline, it is imperative that we discuss the marketing essentials. Marketing essentials are the basic things that every business should have as part of their marketing system.

A plan – This is first on my list for obvious reasons. A well thought out plan allows you to clearly state and focus on accomplishing your business objectives. Having a concrete plan as to how you want to grow your business instills confidence in your investors, partners, employees etc. It gives them as well as yourself a sense of purpose and direction.

A budget – A budget is an approximate estimate of what it is going to financially take to effectively and efficiently run your business. A lot of entrepreneurs usually proceed without a budget and figure "hey if I need the money I will just go out and get it". There's nothing wrong with that attitude because sometimes at the initial outset of a business or startup capital is scarce, but that doesn't necessarily mean that you shouldn't have a budget. Along the way as your business gains traction, potential investors want to see numbers wise what it will take to run your business and make it profitable.

Company Logo – A good company logo is essential because it is your company's first impression to the public and it gives your brand a visual identity in the form of a graphic that people will see, memorize and associate your business with. Case in point, when people around the world even in the remotest places see the Coca Cola logo they know what it is and what it stands for.

Business Cards – Although this essential may seem dated and antiquated, business cards are an extremely practical and convenient form of marketing. They are convenient because you can carry them everywhere you go and hand them out to people instantly. Practical because its recipients can easily place the card in their wallet, pocketbook or pocket and review the information on it later. It saves you and them the trouble of having to manually write down your business's information such as the phone number, name of your company, physical location and website address.

Core message or unique selling proposition – The core message of your company is a very important marketing essential. It will telegraph to the marketplace what you do and how you do it. Your core message should indicate to the marketplace why they should do business with you as opposed to another company.

The way that you get your message across is by creating a unique selling proposition (USP). A unique selling proposition is what sets your products or services apart from your competitors. It is a statement, concept, idea or a way of doing business that tells your potential customers why they should do business with you over someone else. Here are some examples of some famous and great USPs.

Domino's Pizza

"You get fresh, hot pizza delivered to your door in 30 minutes or less or it's free"

M&Ms

"The milk chocolate melts in your mouth, not in your hand"

DeBeers

"Diamonds are forever"

Avis

"We're number two. We try harder"

Wheaties

"The breakfast of champions"

A website – We live in an ecommerce world so it is essential that your business has a website. Not only do people buy things from their computer via the internet, but they also buy and access the internet via their mobile phones. If you don't have a website you are leaving money on the table. When you have a business people expect you to have a website.

A company mobile phone– If you don't have an office (home-based or otherwise) it is best to use a company mobile phone for your business. You don't want to use your personal cell phone for business because it conveys that you are really not that professional, although that may not be the case. In business perception is everything, and what helps mightily with the perception of your business is when someone calls your mobile phone and they are greeted professionally.

Letterhead – When you're marketing your business offline one of the essentials that you should have in your arsenal is a letterhead. A letterhead enables you to send your company's brand out on all of your communications with your customers and vendors. This allows you to build recognition for your brand and also enhances the perception that you are credible and professional.

Email signature – An email signature serves the same purpose of a letterhead the only difference is it is used in your online correspondence instead of by traditional mail. Each business email that you send should include a proper email signature to add credibility to your business.

Mental toughness – I know that you are probably surprise by mental toughness being listed as a marketing essential, but here is the reason for its inclusion. When you are investing money in your marketing some things are going to work and some things are not going to work, that's the reality. When things don't work, you can't fold and succumb to the pressure of that reality, you must either make adjustments to your particular marketing tactic that's not working to make it work or abandoned it all together.

Testing is part of the marketing game and you can't get emotionally wrapped up into the results. Whenever you find yourself becoming unnerved, frustrated or unglued, I want you to think about the perspective and mental toughness that the inventor Thomas Edison exuded when inventing the light bulb.

When Thomas Edison was interviewed by a young reporter who boldly asked Mr. Edison if he felt like a failure and if he thought he should just give up by now. Perplexed, Edison replied, "Young man, why would I feel like a failure? And why would I ever give up? I now know definitively over 9,000 ways that an electric light bulb will not work. Success is almost in my grasp." And shortly after that, and over 10,000 attempts, Edison invented the light bulb.

Creating a Marketing System That Runs On Autopilot

In order to get maximum results from your marketing efforts, it is essential that you systemize your marketing. Why a marketing system? All great businesses run themselves automatically by using a system. When you systemize your business you know exactly what supposed to occur. A prime example of a business that is systemized is McDonald's. They have an ultra successful franchise system that serves billions of burgers and fries to people.

The food taste pretty much the same in every franchise no matter what part of the world the McDonald's is located at. They accomplished this uniformity and consistency by implementing a system that dictates how a burger or fries are supposed to be prepared. Ray Kroc founder of the McDonald's franchise system referred to this systemize process as "The McDonald's Method". The McDonald's method explained to the franchisees such things like how much meat to include in a hamburger, how to cut the fries and how often to clean the restaurant.

McDonald's also has a system when it comes to marketing their business as evident by their slew of T.V. advertisements, billboards, radio ads, newspaper ads, magazine ads, cross promotion with major movies etc. Their marketing is relentless and it never stops. It runs on autopilot 24 hours a day, 7 days a week, and you can't escape it. Just try driving down any major highway, within a short time you will soon see those famous golden arches on the side of the road.

Here's how you would create a marketing system that runs on autopilot. First of all you would identify after testing them, all of the marketing tactics that bring you the best results. By best results I mean the ones that bring you the best return on your investment (roi). Once you have identified the marketing tactics that bring you the best roi, you would then implement a system that ensures that these tactics are employed and repeated all the time.

For example, if you're marketing online and you sent out two discount special offers via email blast and it resulted in an increase in revenue of 30% for that particular month for your business, you would then incorporate and include two discount special offers via email blasts in your marketing system and schedule them to run every month as long as they remain effective. Most autoresponder providers like Aweber and GetResponse offer the scheduling feature for email blasts, so you can have this marketing tactic run on autopilot.

A second example using the offline marketing tactic of direct mail, would be if you mailed out a specific mailing piece to prospects that you obtained from a mailing list and it generated a high conversion rate and increased profits for your business. You would also make sure to include using direct mail in your marketing system. You can set up your direct mail campaign to run on autopilot daily, monthly or weekly or how often you desire.

Another nifty tool that will help you to run your marketing system on autopilot is a website that is designed to prescreen and capture leads as well as make sales. A website is up 24/7 and it works even while you're asleep. For your website to capture leads it must have a form or questionnaire that allows you to capture your website visitor's information. Also you may want to offer a free report as an enticement to get your visitors to fill out the form with their contact information.

Instead of sending your prospects to a full fledge website that offers your products or services, you may want to create a squeeze page. A squeeze page is a one page landing page that has as its main purpose to capture leads. Specifically, the names and email addresses of your website visitors so that you can further follow up with them by sending them emails at different intervals via your autoresponder.

Most people usually don't buy from you the first time that they visit your site. It is only after repeated contacts do they become familiar with you and are comfortable and confident enough to make a purchase. By the way this is usually after around the 4th or 5th contact from you. Since this is the case, rather than lose the prospect, it is best to have their contact information in your autoresponder data base so that you can follow up with them and develop a rapport which will hopefully lead to them to becoming a lifelong customer. As with the scheduling of your email blasts, you can also schedule your autoresponder follow up messages to be delivered on the days and the time that you decide.

An 800 number with a 24 hour pre-recorded message is another tool that you can use that will enable your marketing system to run on autopilot. Having an 800 number with a prerecorded message allows your prospects to anonymously find out about your business and what you can offer them by simply phoning in and listening to a message that's available to them 24/7. It also can be a great way to prescreen your prospects.

A company that I use and highly recommend that is reasonably priced and offers 800 numbers and has an efficient system that will allow you to set up multiple 24 hour pre-recorded messages is freedomvoice.com.

Now if you don't like the idea of directing your prospects to a pre-recorded message, you can use a live answering service that's available 24/7. A company that I highly recommend for this service is patlive.com. You can create your own custom made script that a PatLive receptionist will read from and follow to the T when your prospects or customers call in. Another great service that Pat Live offers is they can take your customers orders right over the telephone. If you have a website that has a simple ordering process they can link directly to your site for easy order fulfillment.

Utilizing the services of a virtual assistant (VA) is another method that you can use to enable your marketing system to run on autopilot. So what exactly is a virtual assistant? A virtual assistant or a VA is generally a self-employed person that provides professional administrative, technical, or creative (social) assistance to clients from a home office.

A virtual assistant can handle any task remotely and they don't have to be "on site". A computer and an internet connection make this all possible. You can communicate instructions for tasks that you need to be completed via email, Skype, instant messaging etc. Virtual assistants are real flexible in terms of time and will work at all kind of hours to suit your needs unlike a regular employee.

I use virtual assistants all the time and they are much more cheaper to use than a regular employee. In fact, in most cases I utilize virtual assistants located in the Philippines to handle a majority of my tasks. The great thing about outsourcing your tasks to the Philippines is that you can hire A level talent at a fraction of the cost or at a discount because of the differences in currencies and economics. A reliable site that I use to hire outsourcers from the Philippines is easyoutsource.com because they offer a credible and reliable service.

Direct Response Marketing

If you are a small business owner or entrepreneur, the type of marketing that you will be primarily using to get customers for your business is direct response marketing. So what exactly is direct response marketing? Direct response marketing is essentially a type of marketing designed to generate an immediate response from consumers. This response can be easily measured and attributed to a specific advertisement that generated the results. Direct response marketing can be delivered through the various forms of media like direct mail, newspaper ads, magazine ads, direct response TV, direct response radio, print advertising, telemarketing, catalogs, and the Internet.

Direct response marketing differs from traditional image marketing done by the large companies like Coca Cola, General Electric, Geico etc. The main purpose of image marketing is to increase awareness of the brand and remind the consumer that you exist in the marketplace.

The idea is that the more the advertisement is seen, the more it seeps into and becomes embedded in the consciousness and sub-consciousness of the consumer which hopefully will result in a purchase. Most of the image advertising that exists today is hard to measure because it doesn't try to elicit an immediate response from the consumer.

For example, although the Geico commercials are quite funny, can the company actually measure the results of their effectiveness in terms of sales? No, they can't. They can't say hey we ran the commercial with the talking lizard and as a result we made X amount of sales. So why would they do it if they can't measure the results? The immediate answer is they have the money to do so. Their marketing budget is huge and they figure it's a sexy way to sell insurance. I mean how many people are going to watch and be interested in a commercial that blandly talks about the benefits of insurance?

Unfortunately, for many small business owners and entrepreneurs they become misguided and try to follow and emulate how "the big boys" do their marketing. Image marketing does not work for the small business owner or the entrepreneur mainly because it requires saturation of the market to reach the consciousness of the market you are trying to target. So save yourself the time, money and energy and don't engage in this form of marketing unless you have millions in your marketing budget. Even then I would think twice about doing it.

Characteristics of Direct Response Marketing

Since we are clear that direct response marketing is the path that you should take, let's discuss the characteristics of direct response marketing.

Direct response marketing is designed to elicit a response – That response could be a visit to your website, a telephone call, the filling out of a form or simply placing an order.

Direct response marketing is trackable - When someone responds to your advertisement, you know immediately which media it came from. For example when I am advertising online using direct response marketing I use a tracking service that allows me to track the clicks and the conversion rate that my banner ads, text ads, and email ads have generated. This allows me to make a great decision based on the results as to what online advertising I should continue to use and which ones I need to eliminate because of their ineffectiveness. The name of the company I use to track my online ads is called Clixtrac.

Direct response marketing is measurable – As mentioned before with direct response marketing you can measure the results.

Direct response marketing targets a specific audience or niche – With direct response marketing you are not trying to market to the entire world because the entire world is not your customer. You are marketing to a specific audience or niche who are more likely to be interested in the products or services that you have to offer.

Direct response marketing has a "call to action" – It instructs the prospect or customer to do something. It demands a response. Here are some examples of call to actions, "visit our website", "fill out this form", "call this toll free number now", "order now and receive a free gift", "act now because this is a limited time offer".

Direct response marketing uses compelling headlines and sales copy – Direct response marketing uses powerful headlines that is primarily designed to attract interest from viewers to read the entire body of your sales copy. That's why newspapers use powerful headlines, to get you to read the rest of the article. Take a look at these two headlines from the Daily Mirror newspaper in England, does it get your attention and entice you to read the rest of the article?

How Can 59,017,382 People Be So Dumb?

This headline perfectly illustrates Britain's reaction to the re-election of President Bush.

Careless Spliffer: George Michael's Cannabis Arrest

This is a really great two-word headline that plays on the George Michael song "Careless Whisper" and a spliff, which is a nickname for a marijuana cigarette.

The headline is usually the biggest typographical element on the page. It's supposed to be the "entry point" into the ad. It's an attention-grabber. It should also be simple enough to get your point across in a limited space. You don't want your headline to be too long or complex. Focus on a core problem or a key benefit of what you are offering. The body of your sales copy should also focus on the benefits and clearly explain to your prospects "what's in it for them?" if they take you up on your offer.

After the body of your sales copy, you have to have as mentioned previously a strong "call to action" that persuades and directs the prospect to take the action that you want them to take. This process that I just briefly described is known as copywriting. Copywriting is the art and science of strategically using words to persuade your intended target to take action. Copywriting is formulaic in nature and its elements consist of a headline, a subhead, body copy, testimonials, an irresistible offer, a call to action and a P.S. at the bottom of the page if you are writing a sales letter to reaffirm your offer or the benefits. I go over copywriting extensively in my book entitled "How To Sell Any Product Online: "Secrets of The Killer Sales Letter"

How to Market Your Business Offline

Now we are going to get into the meat and potatoes of this book, how to market your business offline and online. First we are going to focus on the various ways in which you can market your business offline. I know that we are living in the information age and as a result many business owners and entrepreneurs have gravitated towards the internet and online marketing to reach potential customers. While marketing your business online is a necessity, you can't forget or neglect marketing your business offline. Online marketing and offline marketing should go hand in hand to form a lethal and effective combination. So without further ado here are the various ways in which you can market your business offline.

Direct Mail

Direct Mail – Marketing your business via direct mail is my personal favorite offline marketing tactic because it has been so effective and profitable for me. Direct mail falls under the category of traditional marketing because it has been around for such a long time. Many astute and savvy marketers successfully use direct mail to sell just about every product imaginable at practically every price point.

Advantages of using direct mail in your offline marketing campaign

Direct mail is targeted – you can reach any niche no matter how big or how small by purchasing a mailing list from mailing list brokers who specialize in selling targeted lists in any niche regardless of how obscure it is. You want to sell a knitting kit to women who are 50 years old or older? There's a list available out there somewhere consisting of these types of women buyers. You want to sell pig slop to pot belly farmers? There is also a list out there consisting of these types of farmers. I'm not exaggerating in the least bit.

Direct mail is much more intimate and personal – believe it or not people like receiving mail as long as it's not a bill. If you send something interesting and package it and personalize it so that it doesn't look like junk mail chances are that it will get opened and read which puts you in the position to receive a response. Your message can also be tailored to fit each individual.

People prefer direct mail - according to Infotrends, 69 percent of consumers prefer traditional mail over e-mail for direct marketing.

Direct mail is interactive - Direct mail also offers the opportunity for your prospects or customers to hold your business's message in their hands.

Direct mail can increase your website traffic – you can use direct mail to drive prospects or customers to your website.

Direct mail is easily measurable – you can measure the number of responses, amount of coupons redeemed, donations garnered, the amount of sales generated and the number of telephone inquiries received.

Direct mail produces a higher response rate - Direct mail pieces like catalogs, letters, postcards, brochures, promotional items, etc. produce a higher response rate than email and print ads combined.

Direct mail allows you to expand and reach a larger audience – When you strictly market online, you can only reach the people who use the internet. Direct mail enables you to expand your reach to people who don't use computers or go online.

The Different Formats of Direct Mail

The following is a list of direct mail formats that you can utilize when marketing your business offline:

The Letter

The letter based on my personal experience is the most effective direct mail format. People have no resistance to a letter unless it is junk mail or a bill. In fact, most people sort their mail by the garbage can. They have an A pile, B pile and C pile. The A pile is the mail that they have to open and read now. The B pile is the mail that they can read later and the C pile goes straight in the trash.

Obviously, you would want your letter to make it into the A pile and at all cost avoid the dreaded C pile. The way that you would accomplish this is by making your letter look like it's from "Grandma". It has to be handwritten and that includes the letter as well as the envelope.

I know that you are probably thinking at this point what if I have a ton of letters to mail wouldn't it be kind of tedious to handwrite them all? It most certainly would be and I don't recommend that. What I do recommend is that you use an authentic looking handwriting font and use the mail merge feature on your computer to handle this task.

Also to make it into the "A pile" you should also use live first class stamps, because if you use metered stamps it screams out to your prospects or customers conscious and subconscious mind "junk mail"! The same goes with those computer generated white address labels, so you should avoid them at all costs.

Sequential Follow Up Mailing System

In order to have a super effective direct mail letter campaign that elicits a high rate of responses, you should send out more than one letter to your prospects or customers. In fact, you should create and develop a sequential follow up mailing system that runs on autopilot. You should create a sequential mailing system to generate leads, to follow up with leads, to follow up with customers, to gain a customer back when you have lost them etc.

Another reason why you should mail in a sequential fashion to your prospects and customers is because maybe when you mailed your 1st letter, 2nd letter, or 3rd letter they weren't motivated enough to respond to your offer or they weren't interested in it at that particular moment. However, over time and after a few more correspondences from you they might be motivated to respond. Of course you would have to set your limit as to how many follow up letters you will be sending out.

Nonetheless, repeated mailings allow you to get into the conscious and subconscious mind of your prospects and customers and when they do become motivated to respond to your offer, they will give you a call, visit your website, or respond to whatever your call to action tells them to do. My personal motto is "keep mailing them until they tell you to stop, then mail them again".

In my real estate business I created my own proprietary sequential letter system for mailing to potential motivated sellers of real estate. Here are two examples of a first letter and then 2nd letter follow up to give you an idea of what I'm talking about.

Letter 1

Dear John:

My name is Omar and I would like to buy your house located at 1313 Mockingbird Lane. I am not a realtor. I am a real estate investor who is associated with a group of investors that buy 5–10 houses per month. If your property qualifies, I will make an offer on your house right on the spot guaranteed!!

People sell houses for many reasons:

Divorce, behind on payments, liens, 100% financed, fire damage, foreclosure, bad tenants, vacant house, job relocation, making payments on another house etc.

No matter what the situation, price range, area, or condition of the house. John, I can pay all cash with no contingencies and close in a few days if needed. I will diligently work with you to create the perfect solution for your specific situation. For example, I can buy or lease your house, make the payments, as well as do the repairs. In addition, I will also handle all of the paperwork and make all the arrangements.

Should you have any interest in selling your house quickly and easily at a fair price. Please call me at (201) 555–5555. You can also visit us at www.ourwebsite.com to submit a "property information" form (which takes less than a minute to complete) to get the ball rolling. If you're not interested in selling this property now, please keep this letter for future reference.

Sincerely,

Omar Johnson

P.S.– Remember if your property qualifies I will make you an offer right on the spot.

Letter 2

Hi John,

This is Omar. I wrote to you about 30 days ago in regards to my interest in buying your house located at 1313 Mockingbird Lane. My interest remains strong and I can pay all cash and close in as little as 72 hours if needed.

No matter what the price range, situation or condition of the house, I'm equipped to make an offer right on the spot!! This eliminates the need to deal with banks (I will be paying all cash) or list with a Realtor(they tie up your house for a period of time with the possibility of not selling it)

I can also guarantee a hassle free transaction because I will handle all of the paperwork and make all of the necessary arrangements. To get the ball rolling, simply give me a call at (201) 555-5555 or visit my website at www.ourwebsite.com to submit a "property information" form. This form takes less than a minute to complete and it's free!

Sincerely,

Omar Johnson

P.S. Give me a call at (201) 555-5555 or go to the website ourwebsite.com and fill out the "property information" form to at least find out what fair price I can offer you for your house, you may be in for a pleasant surprise!

The main key to running a successful sequential letter campaign is organization. You must have a database system that allows you to keep track of your prospects/customers as well as the time and dates of your mailings. Trust me, if you don't have this it can get quite confusing and result in chaos. To find a database system that specifically serves your business needs. Just Google "direct mail software programs".

A/B Split Testing

You should create two different letters to mail out in your direct mail letter campaign to test which one yields the best results before you roll out your mailing campaign to your entire list. This is referred to as A/B split testing. Once you have made the determination as to which one performs the best, use that particular letter to mail out to your entire list.

The best way to perform your A/B split testing is by using a sample of 2,000 people on your list. You would send the first letter that you created to 1,000 of those people on your list and you would send the second letter that you created to the other 1,000. In order to get a fair reading as to what letter performs the best you would have to mail out at least 1,000 letters a piece.

Mailing Lists

I mentioned earlier that you can buy a mailing list from a list broker so that you can reach your target market via direct mail. I'm going to now discuss the two types of lists that you can purchase and what to look for and what questions you should ask before buying them.

There are two types of mailing lists, compiled lists and response lists. A compiled list is general information that is gathered from sources such as the yellow pages, directories, and other public domains. For example, a directory of accountants is a compiled list.

Response list on the other hand are lists that consists of people who have taken a specific action like responding to an advertisement or buying a product or service. The great thing about response lists is that they allow you to target and reach individuals who are already in the market for what you offer.

Before purchasing your mailing list from a list broker make sure that you give them the characteristics of the list that you are looking to purchase. For example, a list of dog owners who have purchase puppy chow within the last year are considered to be characteristics of a list.

Here are some questions that you would ask the mailing list vendor:

Does the list consist of people who actually bought something or just inquired about it? I usually choose the list that consists of actual buyers. Why? Because they have shown a willingness to purchase something similar to what I am offering. Also I want to know the dollar amount of the purchase. If I am selling a $500 dollar product, I want a list of buyers who have shown through past behavior that they are willing to spend $500 or more on a product that's in a similar category.

How recent is the list? I want to know how old the list is. I usually purchase what are called "hot lists" because these people have bought something within the last 30 days, so they are more apt to spend money on similar offerings because they are hot for them.

How often is the list updated? You must ask this question to avoid buying a stale list or a list that has a high amount of non-deliverables.

How many people have continued or repeated using the list? Asking this question will help you determine how good the list is.

Once the mailing list broker has satisfied and answered all of your questions you will make your purchase. A word to the wise, you should start out small, most list brokers require that you buy a minimum of 5,000 names. Once this list has proven to be successful, buy another 5,000 names. If your second 5,000 names also prove to be successful only then should you increase your purchase and roll out your letter campaign.

Two excellent resources that you can use to find a specific mailing list for your business are SRDS Direct Marketing List Source and the Oxbridge Communications National Directory of Mailing Lists. You can find these two publications at your local library.

13 Direct Mail Secret Marketing Tactics

The following is a list of 13 direct mail secret tactics that you should incorporate to ensure that your direct mail campaign is a success:

Direct Mail Secret Marketing Tactic #1

To dramatically increase the rate of getting your letters opened and to immediately grab the attention of your prospects simply write these words in red on the front of your envelope: Very Urgent Open Immediately!

Direct Mail Secret Marketing Tactic #2

Give your letter an easy to read appearance by using subheads, underlining, boldfacing, numbering and bullets.

Direct Mail Secret Marketing Tactic #3

Sign your name using blue ink – A 1987 study by Dodd & Markwiese found that a hand signed signature in blue ink increased response by 21%.

Direct Mail Secret Marketing Tactic #4

Always include a P.S. in your letter because it is the most read part of the letter. Strangely enough, people will read the P.S. first before they read the entire letter so it should have urgency, encourage action and give an assurance like a guarantee.

Direct Mail Secret Marketing Tactic #5

Tailor the content of your letter as much as possible. Sending letters that are general are less effective, so it is important that you make the reader feel as though you have taken the time out to specifically make your letters relevant.

Direct Mail Secret Marketing Tactic #6

Give them a deadline- Sometimes people don't act unless prodded to do so.

Direct Mail Secret Marketing Tactic #7

Make it easy for them to respond – Give them several ways to contact you such as by telephone, email, fax or simply by visiting your website and filling out a form.

Direct Mail Secret Marketing Tactic #8

Offer them a bribe – Offer incentives to your prospects and you will be amazed how your conversion rate will increase. My favorite all time bribes that I employed were offering a free vacation to Paris to homeowners who have successfully done business with me and also offering moving money to the homeowner who has sold their house to me as a result of going through the foreclosure process.

Direct Mail Secret Marketing Tactic #9

Use a friendly conversational style when writing your sales letter. Do not use large words or try to sound to "corporate". Write as if you are talking to your best friend. In some cases, the more grammatically correct you try to make your writing, the less effective it will be.

Direct Mail Secret Marketing Tactic #10

Don't make promises that you can't keep. You have to be honest about what you can do for your prospect. Never make false claims or mislead in your sales copy or you will ruin your reputation in the marketplace.

Direct Mail Secret Marketing Tactic #11

You must sell yourself in 6 seconds or less. Therefore you must immediately state the benefits of your offer to avoid losing your prospect's attention. Once you lose their attention your letter ends up in the trash.

Direct Mail Secret Marketing Tactic #12

Don't be afraid to use long copy. Your letter should be long enough to explain all that you have to offer. So don't be afraid to explicitly give the details of the benefits and solutions that you offer. Never be boring and remember if they are truly motivated and are interested, and your story is good, they will read it.

Direct Mail Secret Marketing Tactic #13

Use tear sheet mailings to increase responses – A tear sheet is an article that appears to be torn from a real newspaper. This newspaper article or tear sheet contains relevant information about you and your company.

The reason how and why it works effectively is because a handwritten note or a letter is attached to the newspaper article and sent to your prospect. This handwritten note would say on it "Hey Jim (or whatever your prospect's name is), check this article out".

The chances of your prospect reading the article is very high because he or she thinks it was sent and recommended by someone that they know.

Also, the reason why it works is because your article is printed on authentic 30lb newspaper stock with printing on both sides of the paper and the piece is designed to look and feel exactly like an industry specific edition of a large newspaper.

Postcards

Using postcards is another effective direct mail format and is a great way to contact and stay in touch with potential prospects and customers. Unlike an envelope it doesn't need to be opened! After communicating with potential prospects or customers via letter multiple times, I usually start utilizing the postcard around the 3rd, 4th or 5th mailing. Postcards are cheaper to mail than letters and can usually be printed fairly cheaply through online vendors.

Brochures

Brochures are a great way to get your message across to prospects and customers. I usually send brochures out accompanied by a personal letter. Your brochure should be and is traditionally tri-folded.

When designing your brochure make sure you have a benefit driven headline. In addition, be sure to include your most important points in the places most often read besides the headline like the subheads and caption.

I must reiterate this very important point. Your brochure must convey the benefits. Your potential customer is simply reading your brochure and trying to determine and find out "what's in it for me?"

Self Mailers

Self mailers are direct mail pieces that can be mailed "as is". There is no need for an envelope because they fold into themselves and stay shut with an adhesive tab.

Flyers

Flyers are a fantastic, versatile, easily controlled and economical way of getting your message out to a broad audience. Flyers are in fact so very versatile that no matter what budget you have to start with, even if you feel you are starting out with next to no budget, there is a way to do your flyers that will get your message out there and creating results.

Even with no money set aside, here is an easy way to get started with flyers. What programs do you have on your computer right now that will help you lay out a clear, neat, easy to understand flyer?

From word processing software, simple paint and draw applications, right up to your photo manipulation style software – I'd be surprised if there weren't at least two programs already installed on your computer that would be capable of quickly and easily creating a flyer to promote your business. Sit down with a cup of coffee, have a play with the programs and put together a mock flyer.

The size is up to you. Obviously the smaller your flyer is, the more economical it is for you to produce, but the trade-off is that you are limiting the amount of information you are getting to your prospective clients. A good size is two per page (approx 8 ½ x 5 ½) this way, whether printing them yourself, or when the budget gets expanded to having them professionally done – you are getting twice the amount of flyers as if they were a full standard letter page (8 ½ x 11).

What is even more important than the actual size of your flyer is the message. You don't need to be super fancy with your message. As you come to find in marketing yourself and your business, simple is better. Know the point you are trying to get across and stick to it. Deliver a simple and straightforward message to the person holding the flyer. The whole aim of the exercise is to pique the interest of the person who has received your flyer.

Catalogs

Catalogs showcase a wide range of products in magazine form. Catalogs vary in size dimensions. Common sizes are approximately 6"x 9," 11" x 6" or 8.5" x 11." If you offer a variety of products, then sending out a catalog to your customers and prospects is a great way to fatten up your profits and enhance your bottom line. Catalogs are also a highly interactive form of direct mail.

Dimensional Mailers

Dimensional mailers are basically a step up from brochures. Dimensional mailers are described as any direct mail piece that is not mailed as a flat letter or postcard. Lumpy mail is considered to be dimensional mail. Lumpy mail is aptly named because it is mail that is "lumpy". Lumpy mail usually consists of promotional items and it is highly effective because it is something different that people are not use to receiving as opposed to a traditional letter or a postcard.

Newspaper Advertising

Newspaper advertising is another great marketing tactic that you can use to market your business offline. It is particularly useful if you need to get your message out to your target market in your local area.

There are several different newspaper advertising formats and they are worth investigating to ascertain whether or not they fit with your business model.

Classified ads – Classified ads are a long standing newspaper advertising tradition as many business owners and entrepreneurs have found success using them. If they are crafted right, they can generate instant interest in your business. The appeal of classified ads are they are inexpensive and can serve as a useful testing tool in determining if you have a commercially viable service or product. In addition, they are great for marketing a single product or making a short announcement. Typically, newspapers charge you by the line or by the word.

Inserts – According to the Newspaper Association of America:

* 73% of adults shop by reading newspaper advertising inserts

* 64% of adults prefer to receive coupons in newspaper inserts, more than all media combined

Obviously, according to these statistics newspaper inserts are very popular among adult consumer buyers and if you can find a way to make them work for your business then you should. Inserts are usually put in the weekend paper, with Sunday being the best day for them.

They are typically 8 ½ by 11" or 11 by 17 inches folded in half. Inserts can also be customized. To save on cost, you might want to consider going into an advertising co-op with another business and working out a deal that each company gets a side of the insert.

Display Ads

I'm also a big fan of using display ads because they give you more space to display your message prominently. The majority of your small business owners and entrepreneurs are not even thinking about display advertising because of the following reasons:

1) They think it's too expensive.

2) They think it's only for the big boys.

They are dead wrong with this assumption. Display advertising is only costly if you pay and go by the newspaper's rate card which you will never do as an astute marketer. You will use what is called remnant advertising to get your display ads at a fraction of their cost.

Remnant Advertising

What is remnant advertising? Newspapers, radio, magazines, and television stations sometimes have unsold advertising space available and they need to fill it because if they don't, it is lost or given away for public service announcements or some other non-revenue producing filler. So instead of taking a loss these media outlets will often take far less than their usual retail fees to unload their remnant space.

So before you order any type of media advertisement make sure you inquire about remnant advertising, because not only will you save a great deal of money, you will also get a great bang for your buck.

How to Effectively Use Display Ads

When using display advertising, make sure you use or fill up the entire space that you have paid for with your message. Also make sure that your display ad is appealing, easy to read, scannable and please once again don't leave a lot of white space or blank space in your ad, because after all you did pay for the space so you might as well use it and fill it up with relevant information.

In addition, it would be foolish to use your display space for traditional branding purposes like the "big boys" do with image marketing.

Case in point, have you ever seen those display advertisements for new cars? They have just a few words in the ad that tells the name of the car, some of its features and they show nice pictures of it but they never give you the benefits of owning it.

What's even more stupid is there is nowhere in the ad that tells you how and where to buy it if you actually wanted one. So don't think about traditional branding or putting a big picture of your company's logo and highlighting that you've been in business for 25 years because in this particular case that's a waste of space that can be used to highlight the benefits of what you are offering. Remember the only thing that your prospects or customers care about is once again "what's in it for me?"

You should create your display advertisement to blend in with the format of the newspaper that you are advertising in. The fonts and style should be similar and the secret to this is that your ad shouldn't look like an ad, but it should look like it's a regular article from the newspaper because it is more likely to be read.

The editors at the newspaper will put a little caption above your ad that says "This is an advertisement" to prevent confusion. However, this doesn't matter. Readers consciously and subconsciously program themselves to skip over ads but are attracted to headlines that stand out and the interesting articles that follow. So it is imperative that you make your headline standout and the content of your text interesting.

The whole purpose of your newspaper advertisement is to locate prospects and get them to respond to you. When they have contacted you, it is your job to get their contact information so that you can follow up either by letter, email or a phone call.

Magazine Ads

Magazine ads are another form of print medium that you can utilize to get your marketing message in front of a targeted audience. Magazine advertising has the advantage that the audience demographic is fairly well defined, so your ad can be specialized for the audience that will be seeing it. And there are so many different magazines on so many specialized subjects that there is a wide selection to choose from: just about every kind of business, hobby, or interest you can imagine is probably the subject of a magazine.

In addition to specialty magazines, national magazines like Time and Newsweek usually have regional editions, so you can have your ad appear in a nationwide magazine but only be viewable in your local area.

Whatever type of market you want to target, remember that magazines are everywhere, and a dedicated search will probably find several that will reach exactly the type of prospect you are looking for. It is important to define your intended prospects as specifically as possible, not only to select the appropriate publications but also to design your marketing message with these prospects in mind.

Your skill at designing marketing messages will make this offline marketing tactic work for you, and the success you have with this marketing tactic will improve as your skill at designing marketing messages improves.

Cable T.V.

Cable T.V. can be an effective offline marketing tactic that you can use to reach your targeted audience. Some of the advantages of advertising using Cable T.V. are the following:

* If it is done locally it can be done at a reasonable cost.

*You can target specific neighborhoods and eliminate areas that you don't necessarily want or need to cover.

* You can pinpoint certain programs and time slots to show your ad.

* The low cost of Cable T.V. advertising enables you to frequently repeat your message.

One of the secrets to cutting your cost down in advertising on cable is to run a simple graphic ad with your message on it accompanied by a voice over explaining the product or services that you have to offer.

This voice can be yours or somebody else it doesn't matter. What matters is the effectiveness of the ad in terms of the responses generated. You can run your voice over graphic advertisement in 15 or 30 second commercial slots.

Yellow Pages

The Yellow pages are a great way to market your business offline because it is where a great deal of your potential prospects look to when they need to find a service that will help them. When people have problems that occur they don't sit around and wait for some television commercial to appear in front of them with the solution. Instead they reach for the nearest yellow pages to look for and find companies or services that might help them.

According to the Yellow Page Publishers Association 77% of U.S. consumers use the yellow pages in an average month and over 95% of homes in the United States have a Yellow Pages directory. So this is clearly further proof of why you should use this medium to attract your prospects.

Furthermore, the Yellow Page Publisher Association claims that 68% of consumers look at bigger ads first when considering using a service or product because a bigger ad signifies to them that business has an established reputation. So when you are purchasing your yellow page ad make sure you purchase enough space that will allow you to stand out and get noticed.

Creating an effective Yellow Page Ad

Surprisingly a lot of small business owners and entrepreneurs fail to include the use of yellow page ads in their offline marketing arsenal and if they do have it in their arsenal they don't use it effectively.

The reason why their advertisements are not effective is because they are too busy copying everybody else's ad in terms of style. That's why no matter what category that you look in throughout the yellow pages all the ads look similar. This is a classic case of monkey-see, monkey-do.

So in essence, that means you can't possibly succeed by doing what everyone else is doing! It's not enough to list your company name and logo with a list of services that you offer. It's not enough to say the same slogany things as your competition because your ad will end up looking like a glorified business card that merely proves you belong in the category you chose!

You must always take into account that when it comes to Yellow Pages Advertising, your prospects are going to turn to your category to decide between you... and EVERYBODY else.

The bottom line is, when creating your yellow pages ad all you have to do is utilize the necessary copywriting elements that I've discussed earlier. Just in case you don't remember these elements include the use of a headline, a subhead, body copy, testimonials, an irresistible offer, a call to action, and a P.S. Create your yellow page ad incorporating these elements and boldly state your unique selling position and you will stand out, get noticed, and get the responses that you need.

Bandit Signs

If you don't mind engaging in renegade marketing, bandit signs are a super great way to market your business offline. So what in the heck are bandit signs? Bandit signs are low tech, low cost signs that are mostly printed on corrugated plastic boards and are placed in visible areas where there is some sort of traffic.

They are most likely to be seen planted on the side of the highway or road or nailed to some public utility pole. They are unavoidable and in your commute or when you travel you see them everywhere. They read We Buy Houses For Cash, Stop Foreclosure Now, We Fix Flat Tires, Low Cost Monthly Dental Plan etc.

Although you see them everywhere, bandit signs are aptly called that for a reason. They are by their very nature a little on the questionable side in terms of their legality. Even so, the chances of you actually going to jail for putting them up are slim and none, but if caught doing so you will be fined.

I know the idea of getting fined doesn't get you excited however, if you don't mind being a renegade marketer, you can not and should not dismiss the idea of using them in your offline marketing attack because they are so effective.

But if you want to stay on the safe side of the law I truly understand. There are non-traditional ways of using bandit signs legally.

For example, I make arrangements with store owners in my area to allow me to put my bandit signs in the windows of their stores. Sometimes I am able to accomplish this for free and other times I just simply pay them a small advertising fee. They always welcome this extra cash in their pockets because it adds to their bottom line.

A great company to purchase your bandit signs from is http://www.banditsigns.com. Their service is impeccable and their prices are very reasonable.

Radio

Like newspaper ads, radio is also another form of traditional advertising. When you advertise on radio you must target the right audience and demographics. In addition, you must make sure that your ad is running on a station that people are actually listening to.

The best stations to advertise on are talk radio, Christian radio, sports radio and news stations because these audiences are avid listeners and that is exactly what you need, an audience that is going to listen to your message and respond to it if it applies to their current situation.

As with newspaper, cable t.v. and in general print media, you should always try to obtain the best possible rates when it comes to radio advertising. You shouldn't necessarily try to lock yourself in a time slot because when you talk with your radio advertising sales rep you will discover that this can be quite expensive.

It shouldn't matter if your advertisement runs at 3 a.m. in the morning because there are a lot of insomniacs out there who will be tuning in during that time. Why do you think those T.V. infomercials run late at night or in the wee hours of the morning? Because they know that people will be awake during those times.

To dramatically slash your radio advertising costs, ask the radio stations that you plan to advertise on about their remnant rates.

Car Signs

When you leave the office, or home, or meetings with potential clients – don't leave your marketing efforts behind! Car signs that are attractive, well made and well designed will catch the eye of everyone who passes by.

You'll be promoting yourself and your business everywhere you go. Car signs or, even better, sign-written vehicles and custom paint jobs help to present a sharp and credible business image. Whether you are using the stick-on magnetic car signs or a custom sign job, you'll have made your ordinary vehicle into an almost effortless marketing tool.

Using your car as a constant advertising tool is a cheap, long lasting and highly effective way to get your name, business goals and marketing message across to the public and it will certainly generate instant inquiries because your business's telephone # and location is in plain view for all to see.

Now is not the time to be shy. To make it big as a business owner or an entrepreneur you need to be BOLD, real BOLD. And if that means splashing your name, website and phone number as well as your company's message or something similar along the side of the family car – do it.

But what if you have lingering doubts about having your car stared at by the crowds at the grocery store or you have limited funds for a detailed custom paint job? My answer to this is simply consider magnetic car signs.

Check them out at www.banditsigns.com or www.supercheapsigns.com to get an idea of how impressive and effective these signs can be. As well as the website's mentioned here, there are plenty more both on the internet and sign makers in your local area. Get as much information as you can and ensure that the companies are quoting for vehicle grade magnetic signs.

A lesser grade of magnet won't hold up (or hold on) and will eventually come loose – most likely while you are on the move, meaning you'll never see your valuable marketing tool again. A high quality vehicle grade magnet will hold like glue.

A high quality vehicle grade magnet car sign will cost you approximately $50. A mere $50 to turn your everyday driving into a client education and fabulous marketing tool? An absolute bargain.

But what to say on your magnetic car signs? Keep in mind that more than likely you will have two magnetic signs (one on each side of your car) both bearing the same message. In many ways, the information you used on your bandit signs would work on magnetic car signs.

In fact, so many of the same rules and benefits apply that you can almost think of your magnetic car signs as constantly moving bandit signs. Simple, easy to read and understand will be your goals.

Bold colors will help your message stand out both from the rest of the body of your vehicle, but also the other environmental factors around you. Obviously, you want to be very clear about what you want to do. Of course you are going to include your contact details and company name, but giving the public a broad knowledge of what you do is the ultimate aim of the car sign.

Door Hangers

What if you could get your business's name on the door – and hopefully on the lips – of every home owner in your target areas within a few easy hours of work? It's unlikely that all of their cars were in the parking areas where you distributed your flyers at. They may not have driven past your bandit signs. And as frantically as you have been distributing your fantastic business cards, it's unlikely that everyone has one.

You may have heard that door hangers are an expensive way to promote yourself and your business – and they can be. But, there are ways of sourcing and creating affordable door hanging signs to bring this marvelous marketing tool into the realms of your advertising budget. Door hanger signs give you the opportunity to let your business welcome your potential customers home at their own front door.

Similar to flyers, door hangers are a highly effective way of getting your message to potential customers in a non-confrontational, easily controlled and financially versatile way. Let me clarify. By non-confrontational it means that even though you have left a door hanger on the front door, the potential customer still has the control over the situation to pick it up and read it. They can do this in their own time at a time that works for them – and feeling in control of their situation is a mental state that most people long for and that includes your prospects and your customers.

By easily controlled I mean that you have a much stronger control on who is receiving your door hangers. You know that this is a potential prospect that you would like to target and you also know that your information arrived. A great place to purchase your door hangers from is http://www.doorhangers.com and in the past I paid only $284 for 5,000 door hangers.

But what should you say once you get your business on the front door of a potential prospect? Exactly what we've been talking about so far. YOUR message. What you do and the benefits that you offer as well as your contact information. Door hangers can carry a large amount of information and still have plenty of room for your contact details.

It is entirely possible to make your own door hangers on a budget. Many of the specialty paper stores will carry a range of perforated papers designed for printing at home. Most of the range will be business cards, but it is possible to find and purchase pre-perforated door hangers.

Most come perforated in a way that will create three separate door hangers from a 8 X 11.5 inch letter page. Should your local paper supplier or stationary store not stock the paper, a quick search on the internet should supply you with a large range of online stores who can provide it for a good price plus delivery. The papers can then be printed to on your normal printer, whether it is a laser, ink-jet or multi-function machine.

Choosing where you would like to distribute your door hangers is a straight forward matter. After looking at your research, decide whether you would like to visit individual houses or whether you are prepared to do the footwork or employ others to do so and get your door hangers out to entire neighborhoods. Much like flyers, you can choose to do all of the distribution yourself. If you're on a tight budget you can rope in the family or friends (bribe them with a lunch date if you need to) to help out for an afternoon, or employ a small team of college or high school students who will happily work for cash on a per-hour basis.

Coupons – ValPak Marketing

So, we've got you thinking about starting a mass offline marketing campaign for your business. There is another form of mass marketing that you see nearly every day, at an affordable cost that has the potential to reach thousands of prospects at a time! What is it? Coupons and coupon mailers! Like business cards, these tiny gems are a fantastic way of getting your business's name and message into thousands of homes – but with coupons, you can find companies that will put them there for you!

Using coupons are a fantastic idea for many reasons. No doubt you've seen thousands of these little advertising jewels over the years, but it is really surprising how often a small piece of advertising delivered directly to a person's home can strongly influence them to respond to your call to action.

But how to get these coupons out into the wider world? A great idea is consider becoming involved in coupon mailers. You know what they are! The envelope stuffed full of coupons that you either receive in the mail or delivered like catalogs to your doorstep. Produced by a wide variety of companies, the coupon mailers contain a vast array of businesses and offers, but they can and most often are targeted to a particular area or zip code.

I should break this to you now. A lot of your coupons will become trash very quickly. Many people either don't open their coupon mailers, or flick through to quickly see if any appeal to them right now – and any that don't, end up in the trash can. This should in no way discourage you. This form of offline advertising can be very profitable.

So, how do you make coupons work for your advertising budget? The good news is, coupons can fit into just about any budget due to their amazing versatility. You won't need to wait until you are raking in the big dollars to make good use of them!

It's hard to talk about coupons without mentioning www.valpak.com as a market leader in creating and distributing local coupons and coupon mailers. I highly recommend looking them up and seeing what they are all about. Valpak is a simple way of getting started with coupon mailers, all in one easy step. Valpak will also help you design an effective coupon for distribution, though of course you can design your own.

In using coupons to promote your business, you have found a low cost, easily tailored way of getting your message and details to thousands of potential customers without any 'leg work' from yourself. Your offer can be easily targeted by the distributing company who can and will aim your coupons to set markets, zip codes, cities or even states. They can even vary the version of your coupon to make sure the most relevant information is going out at all times. In short, you NEED to investigate coupons as a truly viable marketing tool for your business. You won't be disappointed.

Outdoor Advertising

At some point in your life, maybe as a child, did you dream of having your name in lights? I did. Wait a minute ... I still do. And I do get my name in letters three feet high on a regular basis! How? I'm certainly no movie star, but I've got a fantastic marketing tool working for me. Billboards.

Billboards are quite literally the biggest way of getting people to sit up and pay attention to your business. Typical billboard sizes are 14 by 48 feet, 12 by 24 feet (also known as 30 sheet) and 5 by 11 feet (8 sheet). It is only common sense to realize that it is the largest billboards along our freeways that grab the attention of motorists/pedestrians and give your business the highest levels of exposure. As the size of your billboard diminishes, so does the level of attention it grabs, meaning your message will be reaching fewer people.

You will also need someone to design your billboard for you. Obviously, this is NOT a job your home printer can help you with. That said, have a strong idea of how you would like your billboard to look. Have sketches, or photos of billboards that you have seen that caught your eye. Remember, if a marketing idea worked on you, the same idea could be working for you. Any of the advertising agencies should be able to point you in the right direction for a designer for your billboards. Alternatively, most of the billboard companies have their own in-house designers who can help you with your design. Having the designers at the billboard company draw up your billboard design will almost always work out to be the economical option when compared to the designers recommended by advertising agencies.

Should you be going all out (and good on you if you have the budget to do it) studies have shown that billboards with movement are even greater at attracting the attention of the audience than even the largest billboards. There are types of billboards that have rotating panels, twirling ribbons or some movement of lights. As I'm sure you can guess, this does drive the price of the billboard up considerably, but given its higher success rate it is worth asking about.

Another thing to remember in choosing your billboard is to study the traffic counts and demographics. Any reputable agency or company supplying billboards should have these statistics available in order to show you how effective the site you are choosing is.

It is a good point to remember that your billboard is not one of your high detail advertising means. It is simply there for impact and to reinforce the messages you've been sending out with all of the other advertising tools we've been talking about. Keep in mind that the audience for your billboard is almost 100% on the move so keep the sign clear, brief but eye catching.

You will soon see the massive price variations between different billboard companies, and then between the sizes of billboards and features. And one of the greatest challenges to getting a billboard at a price that doesn't break your advertising budget is location. Prime advertising spots are miniature real estate gold! You'll soon see that the more prime the location, the higher your budget would need to be to make it possible. Make sure you actually visit the locations offered to you. You might be surprised that some of the less expensive advertising locations are attracting enough traffic or foot traffic to justify the expense.

If you received the traffic counts and demographics from the billboard companies, you'll be able to see that successful billboards are seen by thousands of people each day. Once you have a cash flow working positively for your business, take the opportunity to get this medium working for you and enjoy the moment while you sit back and wait for the calls or responses to come in.

I love billboards. I think that there are few greater ways of letting people know that you are in business and mean business than a forty foot sign screaming it at them as they wait in traffic! That said, I can in no way pretend it is an economically feasible option for a business that's just starting out. Billboards are pretty much out of the realm of the beginners. But don't be discouraged. Be inspired. As your business grows, remember to set money aside and grow a healthy advertising budget to make your billboard dreams a reality in the near future!

If I have inspired you by explaining the amazing potential benefits of outdoor billboard advertising but there is just no way of making it happen with your business's current advertising budget, don't lose heart. There is a way that you can harness many of the same benefits at a much more affordable price. Bus Stop and Bench signs!

Bus Stop and Bench Signs

Just like billboards, bus stop bench signs are not for the meek and timid. While you might not be able to afford the giant three foot lettering that a billboard can offer you, we can aim for half a foot for a tiny fraction of the cost!

Bus stop signs are an incredibly high visibility method, especially in higher pedestrian traffic and built-up areas. Like a billboard, your bus stop bench sign can be providing your business with a 24 hour a day, 7 day a week level of distinctive advertising exposure. All this and they are surprisingly affordable as well. And because the cost is so much lower than that of a billboard, you have more freedom (and more inclination) to change your message on a more regular basis, or you can utilize the more expensive features such as photos or custom designed logos.

The benefits of bus stop bench signs lie in the ingenious way in which they can get your message to your audience. The fact that there are just so many bus stop benches to choose from means that you can customize the placement of your signs to a particular area or to a transit line that directly affects the demographic you are attempting to reach.

Bus stops, by necessity, are almost always in places of high pedestrian traffic and other busy areas. As such, you can guarantee a large number of people will be passing your sign each day, much the way you know a billboard will be passed by thousands on the freeways and major roads on which they are placed. Also, the people who pass by the bus stop bench sign are likely to be walking a regular path to shop or their workplace – people passing by regularly are bound to take notice of your signs.

A rough average on the amount of time that people spend waiting for a bus is ten or fifteen minutes. They have to wait for their bus. They are a captive audience. Your bus stop bench sign can be holding the attention of these passengers at a time when there is very little else in the vicinity to be occupying their minds. Also, rather than a billboard that needs to get its message out in the brief moments as a motorist passes, once your bus stop bench sign has caught the eye of a passenger, he or she will almost always have time to read more information and copy down your contact details to call you when they get home.

Also, I've mentioned that bus stops are in built up areas. This means that motorists driving past can also get the benefits of seeing your signs. This is especially obvious at earlier or later times when there are less people at the bus stops.

The bus stop bench signs will be more expensive than the smaller disposable advertising and marketing materials that we have been discussing so far. But many of the companies that organize the placement and care of these signs make this a more affordable option by breaking down the fee into a per month or per week charge. Obviously, the charges vary from place to place and most likely, from company to company.

Some will require you to sign an ongoing contract with them for a set period of time, whether it is three months right up to two years. As with billboards it is highly important to get the statistics about any sites that you are interested in to make sure that they have a traffic/pedestrian flow that makes the money you are spending a viable outlay for the rewards it will yield in return.

Neighborhood Bulletin Boards

Spreading your business literature via neighborhood bulletin boards is a great way to target potential customers for your business because believe it or not people actually read these bulletin boards. I consider this to be a guerrilla marketing technique because it requires very little money to do and it is done primarily in the field. On the battle field I've should of said because it is almost equivalent to hand to hand combat.

One way to get your message on neighborhood bulletin boards is by distributing fliers on various bulletin boards in the neighborhood. Neighborhood bulletin boards are often found in various local businesses and public locations. If you are spending time in your target area looking for leads and keeping a pulse on the neighborhood, you are likely to spot a variety of locations that will support this type of advertising.

If your target neighborhood is the type of area that has laundromats, for example, these are good to note because they almost always have bulletin boards that get seen regularly. Check other businesses and stores as well as government buildings as well.

To reiterate the greatest benefit of using this particular medium as an offline marketing tactic is it is both inexpensive and targeted, appearing as it does directly in front of your prospects where they live, so it can get your marketing message in front of people who live in your neighborhood for fairly cheap. Needless to say, the more bulletin boards your advertisement is on the more ubiquitous your message becomes.

Community Events

Something that you should always be looking for as a marketer is opportunities to get yourself and your business within view of the public. This is because a lot more business deals are going to find their way to you the more people know who you are. If your community has any public events that can provide such an opportunity to get noticed you should be aware of them and be ready to act.

Any event that will allow you to mingle with the public and market your business is something that you should investigate; examples include street fairs, festivals, sporting events, parades, or any event where you can set up a booth for your business.

Your personal presentation skills, which are important for networking techniques in general, are crucial when it comes to appearing in public and interacting with community members. The better you become at making a favorable impression and delivering your marketing message in person the better the results you will get from applying this technique.

Being organized and systematic about following up with relevant leads that find their way to you is crucial if you don't want the experience to go to waste, as is keeping up with events in your community and organizing your presentation, whether it includes some sort of a display or is limited to just you giving your sales pitch to as many people as possible. These events may be free or they may have a charge for participation or setting up a booth. You will have to check what is available in your locality to get precise figures.

Neighborhood Publications

As you become more and more familiar with your target market you will become aware of various neighborhood organizations that publish newsletters and other publications. These types of organizations usually sell advertising space to local businesses, which can add to your arsenal of techniques for reaching your target market with your marketing message.

Examples of these types of organizations abound: clubs like Kiwanis and Rotary, Bar associations, schools, churches, sports clubs, hobby groups, and business associations, to point out just a few. Look for these types of organizations in your area, and contact them to ask about advertising in their newsletter. If you happen to be a member of any of these organizations yourself, you should probably start with that one. You might not get a large volume of leads with this method, but the ones you do get should be qualified and cost-effective. As an added benefit, having your ad seen in many of these publications will add to your positive image in the neighborhood.

Finding neighborhood publications is a skill you can improve at with practice, as is designing a marketing message that is compelling to your target market. As you get better at these skills you will have better success with this method. You should have systems in place by the time you get started for placing the ads, answering the calls you receive from them, and tracking the leads that you obtain this way. The rates for this type of advertising will vary widely, but you can expect it to be easily affordable.

Partnership Marketing

A great way to use leverage to grow your business as well as extend your marketing's reach is through partnership marketing. Partnership marketing is simply aligning yourself and your business with other like-minded organizations and businesses to reciprocally expose your brand to one another's customers and provide added value to your own existing customers. The following are ways in which you can form partnerships and strategic alliances.

How to Market Your Business Offline by Using Your Local Chamber of Commerce

Marketing your business utilizing your local chamber of commerce is a great way to form partnerships that will enable you to grow your business and enhance your profits. So what exactly is a chamber of commerce? A chamber of commerce is a form of business network, e.g., a local organization of businesses whose goal is to further the interests of businesses. Business owners in towns and cities form these local societies to advocate on behalf of the business community.

The advantages of joining your local chamber of commerce are the following:

- **It builds credibility** - Over 60% of consumers are more impressed by a business that holds membership in a local chamber. This means that consumers are more likely to do business with a member versus a non-member.

- **Networking Opportunities** –Being a member exposes you to various networking opportunities. When you are a member of your local chamber, you will be invited to the several luncheons that they have throughout the year. It will take about five meetings worth of time; but, in no time you will be exchanging valuable information with other chamber members so that you can use each other's services. Networking also positions you to do possible joint ventures and form strategic alliances which will enable you to grow your business rapidly and geometrically.

- **Marketing and Advertising Opportunities** – Once you join your local chamber of commerce your business is usually listed in both their online and offline directory which gives you maximum exposure around the clock. Members also are offered special advertising and marketing opportunities to reach more customers, such as local event sponsorships and expos.

- **Connection with the local community** – The chamber of commerce has a direct connection to the local community and that includes local businesses as well as consumers. The chamber usually builds a rapport and strengthens its' bond with the community by sponsoring community events or holding educational seminars that are primarily designed to inform the community about the various products and services that are offered by the chamber's members.

The costs of chamber membership can range anywhere from $150 to $600 per year, depending on where you live and the type of membership you seek. Rather than seeing this simply as a business expense, you should view it as a necessary investment that will pay immediate and long term dividends in the form of more customers, increased sales, brand awareness and the establishing of goodwill in the community.

How to Market Your Business Offline by Using a Referral Program

As the owner of a business, you want your first priority to be customer satisfaction. When your customers are satisfied, they have a tendency to refer your products or services to their friends and family, thus increasing your base of customers. Research and studies have shown that one of your greatest means of obtaining new customers is via your current ones. Developing a customer referral program allows your customers to act as ambassadors for your company. This works well, especially for companies that handle customers on a daily basis.

Marketing your business offline with a customer referral program is much easier than you might think. There are several important things you must consider, such as creating an awareness about the referral program among your current customers, educating them about the program, giving rewards for any leads, and the maintenance of valuable customer service and support. This is an amazing channel that you should not be missing out on.

Thus, you have to invest time in developing a customer referral program that will be both sound and effective. It must be one that will encourage your existing clientele to want to spread the word about your products or services. This is the same as creating a huge sales force that can promote your company within your own community. The following are some of the key components of a successful customer referral program.

Rewards

To run a successful referral program, a rewards system must be implemented for all those who decide to participate. To begin, you must define the expectations; in other words, those types of actions that will enable a customer to reap the rewards of the program. There are some businesses that have rewards for every new lead, while others only reward those leads that end in a sale.

You can also consider offering incentives, such as cash rewards or discounts on future or existing orders. If you have customers that refer large quantities of business to you, you can even offer products or services that are distinctly for those who do so. Other incentives can be gift certificates or even free or discounted tickets to special programs or events within the community. To make your referral program as effective as possible, you must converse openly regarding the incentives and make a speedy delivery of those incentives when customers successfully generate referrals for you.

Create Awareness

You must explicitly convey to your customers that you are implementing a referral program and you are seeking their assistance in helping you locate new business. By not asking for referrals from an existing clientele, you are missing out on some of the best referrals that you can obtain. It is important for you to educate your customers on how they can go about giving you referrals and how and when they can expect to receive their rewards for doing so. You can send emails as reminders to your existing client base explaining the methods for offering referrals. You can also keep complete up-to-date details of the referral program on your website and all of your social media profiles.

Quality and Service

In order to truly benefit from such a program, it is crucial that you offer top-notch customer service. When you have a team of happy, satisfied customers working for a common goal, you will find that this is the most effective means of a sales force that you have. There isn't anyone that doesn't like a well-deserved reward now and then, and the types of rewards that you offer will motivate people to act. Your customers will think of ways that they can continue to reap the benefits of your referral program.

How to Market Your Business Offline with Strategic Alliances

A business does not operate in isolation, and there is not one target audience that is unique to one specific business. If you are seeking a way to give your customers a little something extra, it can make perfect sense to take a look at businesses that are complimentary to your own. For example, if you run a trendy clothing store, you can be most certain that your customers are not only interested in clothing, but appearance and grooming, as well. There is a very strong possibility that there are very similar businesses in the vicinity of your own that offer complimenting services, such as hair salons or nail studios. You can use this to your own advantage by forming strategic alliances, or partnerships, with these other businesses. You are not only adding value to your current customers; but, you are also doing something that will enable you to find new clientele at the same time.

Setting up a Strategic Alliance

- Think about the businesses in your local area that could compliment the products or services that you already provide. It is a good idea to research those companies to find out their reputations in the vicinity and how well they value their own customers.

- Consider the types of products or services that these other companies offer and if these products or services would be something that your own customers would consider to be valuable to them. Think about your clients' possible interests and see if there are businesses that would complement those interests that you could then align your company with.

- Approach possible businesses with an idea of how they would be helping their own customers by giving them something valuable, as well. It is not about them promoting your business; in essence, it is about you promoting each other's businesses. You must explain that their customers will appreciate having something of value and it will only increase that company's customer loyalty.

- When you offer something to the other company's customers, it should be something that is free, such as a gift or a certificate for $50 or $100 that they may utilize towards a purchase in your store.

- Take time to explain to the other company that an alliance such as this is a win-win-win, really. You will come away from the transaction hopefully with new clientele, the other company will do the same, and in the end, the customers are happy because they are being rewarded to shop where they normally would anyway.

Some businesses are wary when it comes to strategic alliances, and there is good reason why. By aligning with other businesses, you are essentially putting your reputation on the line. This is why it is so important to first research the potential companies that you are considering as potential partners. You must be open-minded and exhibit a certain level of trust in the other company in order for this type of alliance to go as planned. If you work together, both businesses will soon see the benefits of a strategic alliance.

How to Market Your Business Offline Using Networking Groups

A networking group is basically when people of similar professional or business interests or goals come together to share their knowledge, experience, and expertise. Members of the networking group benefit by sharing industry and non industry related contacts that will possibly help other members gain access to key individuals that they might not have had access to under any other circumstances. You will find that there are several advantages to becoming a member in a professional networking group. The most obvious advantage is more business. Here are other advantages that you gain by using this offline marketing tactic:

Quality Leads

Leads that come from networking groups are usually quality leads. They are usually quality leads because the person that is referring those leads to you usually has a personal or business relationship with the person or business that they are referring to you. In fact, they usually have an intimate understanding of their particular needs and how you can possibly fulfill them.

Get the Customers You Consider Out of Your League

There are, no doubt, clients that you wish you had but, for whatever reason, you feel you can't or won't get them. Usually this is because these clients are out of reach. The number of people in your networking group increases the chances of you obtaining these clients that you feel are out of your league. The one thing that can make these clients accessible is a direct referral from an individual that they already know and trust.

Expanded Business Opportunities

When you are a member of a networking group you have access to people that are involved in a wide range of fields. This presents the opportunity for you to expand your business in other areas you might not even thought of. It also allows you to market your products or services to other niches and extend your marketing's reach.

How to Market Your Business Offline with Sponsorships

A sponsorship is basically putting your financial wherewithal behind a cause, event or initiative. It is a great way to establish goodwill, connect with others and expose your brand to the public. There are many ways that you can use sponsorships as a marketing tool. You can sponsor little league teams, community events, walk- a-thons, marathons, charitable causes or fundraising events.

When you sponsor an event one of the privileges of doing so is you get the opportunity to advertise your business name or logo directly to the people who are participating or are attending the event. Another privilege is you get to hand out promotional items such as t-shirts, stickers and other like items emblazoned with your company's name on them.

The following are the things that you should consider before sponsoring an event:

Establishing your goals or objectives - You must establish your goals or objectives before deciding who or what to sponsor. What exactly do you want to achieve by sponsoring an event? Is it more sales? Is it more brand awareness? Do you want to build loyalty with your existing customers or do you want to reach a whole new raft of customers?

Choosing who or what to sponsor – When you are a sponsor you are associating yourself and your good business name and reputation with the particular event that you are sponsoring, so you have to make sure that the people that are associated with it are reputable. You have to also make sure that the event is aligned with your company's values and core principles. For example, if you were in the business of "healthy living" you wouldn't sponsor a pizza eating contest.

Also when choosing who or what to sponsor you want to make sure that event reaches your target market because if it doesn't what would be the point? You would be just wasting your marketing dollars. Reaching your targeted audience is very important because these are the people who are more likely to purchase your products or services.

Knowing exactly what you receive in return – It makes perfect sense that you know what exactly you will receive in return for sponsoring an event. It has to be a win/win scenario. It would be ideal if you can sponsor an event that offers benefits even after the event is long over with.

Event Marketing

Right on the heels of partnership marketing and another formidable way to market your business offline is through event marketing. Event marketing is the process of marketing your business or your products or services through a themed occasion or exhibit. Usually the best way to gain new business or interact with your targeted audience is by "taking it to the streets" and engaging with them face to face. Event marketing allows you to do just that. It also allows you to provide a memorable experience to others which will be associated with your brand. The following are ways in which you can market your business via events:

How to Market Your Business Offline Using Workshops

A seminar, or workshop, can attract new clients and customers. Your workshop can be informational or instructional in content, and this is a great way to get your name out into the public.

You will receive so many benefits from holding workshops. Your future opportunities and income level will far outweigh whatever time or effort you expend planning your workshop and any anxiety that you may feel about speaking to the public. The following are some of the top reasons why you should plan a workshop.

1. **It positions you as an expert in your niche.** People enjoy working with experts. The media will consult with experts. How do you earn the title of expert? By educating people and sharing your knowledge with them.

2. **It helps you learn more about your customers and potential clients.** It tells you what their wants and needs are. By holding a workshop, you can better find out what exactly your customers or potential customers want or need in person which eliminates any and all guess work because you are hearing it straight from the source. You can also help your workshop attendees to understand your products or services better in case they have misunderstood somewhere along the line as to what you actually provide and how it will benefit them.

3. **It increases brand awareness.** Informative workshops brings awareness to your brand to people that might have never heard of you or your business before and if they are

already familiar with you and your business, it reinforces and reminds them that you are in the marketplace and are ready to service their needs.

4. **It can create an additional income stream.** As you are preparing yourself for your workshop, you will likely be creating handouts and worksheets for your participants. These materials can be reworked into books, workbooks, home study courses, video and audio in the format of CDs or mp3 files. You can then offer these products for sale to people attending the workshop as well as those individuals who could not attend or prefer an alternate way of learning.

How to Market Your Business Offline Using Contests

Contests are a great and fun way to market your business. They are also a great way to create brand awareness, and customer loyalty. They are ideal because they are relatively inexpensive to run and they help create "a buzz" for your business, since it is only natural that people spread the word and tell others about your contest. The following are the steps you should take when creating a contest for your business.

1. **Brainstorming for ideas** – What kind of contest do you want to have? Do you want to have a sweepstakes? Do you want to have a contest to see who comes up with the best idea for a new product or service? As you can imagine the possibilities are endless. Whatever contest you decide to create is entirely up to you, but you want to make sure that it appeals to your targeted audience and enhances your business.

2. **Have a budget** – Once you decide on what type of contest you are going to have you should create a budget for it. Like I mentioned before contests are relatively inexpensive to run, so you don't want to get carried away with your costs.

3. **You have to have a prize or several prizes** – Let's face it the main reason why people enter contests are to win prizes. Once you have determined your budget for your contest make sure you have properly allocated money for the purchase of your prizes. I say prizes because you can have a first place winner, a second place winner etc. for the contest that you are running.

4. **Setting it all up** – Once you have decided on your prizes it is now time to actually set your contest up. You have to set up your system to track your contest participants, the results and a way to make sure all of the rules of the contest are being followed. You also have to set a time frame when your contest will begin and end.

5. **Promote, promote, promote!** Once you have set everything up, your last step will be to make people aware of your contest. This is also publicity for your company. Create postcards, flyers, use direct mail, newspapers or local radio ads to get the word out about your contest.

6. **Pick a winner.** – When your contest is over and you have a winner make sure that you gain mileage from that winner. Announce them with much fanfare as you did your contest because this will attract more attention for your business. Your winner will also more than likely spread the word to others about winning your contest.

How to Market Your Business Offline Using Educational Seminars

You can market your business offline by either hosting your own educational seminar or participating in an educational seminar hosted by another entity. I particularly like educational seminars because you can enlighten and educate your seminar attendees on a particular subject or topic that is of interest to them and then up-sell them.

For example, if you were in the self-help industry you can put on a free educational seminar for your customers that shows them how to improve their lives or reach their goals. Once you have provided that value, at the end of the seminar you can up-sell them to a monthly or yearly membership plan, offer educational materials for purchase, or offer coaching and consulting services. To use educational seminars as a successful offline marketing tool, here are some of the things that you need to consider.

Identifying your business objectives – What do you want to accomplish by hosting or participating in an educational seminar? Is it to make immediate sales or it is strictly for lead generation purposes?

The message you have to deliver – Before hosting or participating in an educational seminar, you want to make sure you have a strong message and clear value to deliver to your attendees, because if it's not something of value people will be disappointed and your business's credibility will suffer.

Picking an appropriate topic – You must make sure that the topic or subject is relevant to the audience that you are speaking to. This of course is easy when you're hosting and promoting your own educational seminar however, when it involves another entity's educational seminar before you decide to participate you want to make sure that your targeted audience will be attending.

"Call to action" - Educational seminars should close with a clear "call to action". You must define the next step your attendees should take. Your "call to action" could be in the form of a purchase or a sign up where your attendees are providing you with their contact information for further follow up and interaction.

Selection of your venue – The venue that you choose to hold your educational seminar should be in a convenient and easily accessible location and it also should be professional and comfortable.

How to Market Your Business Offline Using Speaking Engagements

Speaking engagements are a great way to bolster your marketing however, most business owners and entrepreneurs shy away from it because they have a fear of public speaking. In fact, some studies have suggested that public speaking ranks right up there with the fear of death. When you're afraid to speak in front of the public you miss out on opportunities to promote your business and grow your customer base.

If you have a fear of public speaking here are some tips that you can use to overcome your fear:

Preparation – The more prepared you are the more confidence you will have to deliver your speech. The way that you prepare is through practice. Once you have written your speech and prepared the materials that you are going to present, practice daily on the delivery of your speech. As the saying goes "practice makes perfect", and the more you practice the less nervous you will be.

Don't worry about making mistakes – If you constantly worry that you will make mistakes when giving your speech this will produce unwanted anxiety before your speaking event and may produce a self fulfilling prophecy scenario. So don't worry about making mistakes and remember that if you do make a mistake on stage, you have the ability to correct it. It is not the end of the world.

Be yourself – When giving your speech just be yourself and it will work out fine. Don't try to imitate someone else's personality because it will come off as being unnatural or you may be viewed as a phony. If you are naturally a passionate and engaging person be that to your audience and don't tone down your presentation because you feel that the audience that you are speaking to won't appreciate your style.

Get rid of unwanted stress – Eliminate any stress out of your life that will have an impact on your performance. You need to have a clear mind and relaxed body to deliver an optimum performance.

There are 3 main reasons why you should consider speaking engagements as an offline marketing tactic:

1) **Visibility** – It gives you instant visibility, it associates a face and voice with your business. Remember the old adage "seeing is believing?" Well it applies here. The bottom line is speaking at an event gives you exposure to potential clients and referrals.

2) **Credibility** – When you speak at an event it gives you credibility and "expert" status. It also allows you to partake in questions and answer sessions where your expertise in on full display.

3) **Profitability** – Speaking at an engagement can bring you instant revenue. For example, if you offer products your audience can purchase them at the end of your speech or at the close of the speaking engagement.

How to Market Your Business Offline Using Trade Shows

Trade shows are a great way to sell your product or services and also are great for networking with other businesses in your industry. A trade show is essentially an event where goods and services in a specific industry are exhibited and demonstrated to other businesses as well as the general public.

Here are some benefits and advantages of using trade shows to market your business:

Opportunity to introduce a new product – A trade show is the perfect opportunity for you to introduce a new product to the marketplace. There are usually media present during trade shows and if your product is impressive and stands out it will garner media attention which will in effect expose your product and your business to many more people.

Interaction – A trade show enables you to interact with potential clients, customers, and industry vendors.

Staying abreast of the competition – A trade show will probably include a lot of your competitors and that makes it the perfect opportunity to stay abreast of what they are doing. You can use the trade show as form of intelligence gathering.

Targeted market – A trade show is a great way to reach your targeted market. The people that are attending the trade show are exactly the type of people you want to attract and sell to.

Direct selling – This is one of the big reasons why you should use trade shows, to directly sell your products to the market. Sales conversions are usually higher because you have a chance to interact with your potential customers and offer demonstrations on how they will benefit from purchasing your product.

In concluding this topic, trade show events can be a worthwhile investment however, you must choose the ones that are right for your specific industry and goals.

How to Market Your Business Offline by having an Open House

An open house is not only used to show people real estate, it can also be used as a marketing tool for businesses that are in other industries as well. If appropriate, maybe your business can benefit from having an open house? An open house attracts customers and it allows you to showcase your products and services to gain new customers and interact with existing ones. You can even utilize your open house to thank customers.

There are many ways that you can use an open house to propel your business and here are a few of them:

You can use an open house to distribute your company literature – This is an unobtrusive way to distribute your company's literature to the public. You are not mailing them anything or bombarding them with harassing phone calls to get their business, you are simply inviting them to the friendly confines of your place of business so that they can become familiar with you and what you have to offer. A word to the wise, offer refreshments and believe it or not this will entice people to come through your doors.

You can use an open house to connect with people aesthetically – If your place of business is aesthetically appealing, it gives your open house attendees additional confidence in making their decision to do business with you. So if you have been awarded plaques or other types of awards for your great service, make sure you have these on full display. It will also help a great deal if you have testimonials available from past and present customers recognizing your great service. A super clean and aesthetically attractive place will make a long lasting and indelible impression on the minds of your open house attendees.

You can use an open house to find out first-hand the problems that people need solved – People will attend your open house for various reasons, but one of the main reasons why they are attending is because they are looking for a solution to a particular problem. For example, if you had a vacuum cleaning business the people that attend your open house are perhaps looking to get their residence or place of business cleaned. They are at your open house to evaluate you to see whether or not you are the solution for them.

An open house gives you the opportunity to directly ask your customers or prospects what problems they are experiencing. This puts you in the perfect position to offer solutions as well as gain their confidence and business.

How to Market Your Business Online

We live in the information age and presently there are more people online than ever, including your target audience and potential customers that you seek out for your business. Needless to say, in order to reach your target audience and potential customer base, you must have a strong online presence in terms of marketing.

Anyone who is engaged in business should be aware of the importance and efficiency of online marketing. However, marketing your business online is also very challenging with so many factors to consider. To guide you I am going to break down the major online marketing platforms one by one and get into the specifics, starting with social media.

Social Media

How to Market Your Business Online Using LinkedIn

LinkedIn is one of the smaller social media outlets, yet it is one of the best platforms that you can use to market your business. The best part of LinkedIn is that it specializes in professional and business profiles. People who use LinkedIn aren't after funny pictures of cats. They are looking to network with other professionals in their industry.

You should be using LinkedIn to establish your business as a credible and reliable business in your industry. It is a great way to establish your own credibility and build a network of people who work in similar areas. LinkedIn is advertised primarily as a way for individuals to make professional connections and market themselves, but it is also a very useful tool for businesses to market their services as well.

Why Networking With Other Professionals Matters

You might be thinking to yourself that there is no point to marketing to other professionals in your industry, because after all they are after the same pool of customers that you are. However, this logic isn't always true. Networking can be an effective marketing tool, but only if you do it the right way. The key is to market to professionals who aren't directly competing with you.

For example, if you are a wedding photographer, you should create a network of videographers, wedding planners, and other wedding professionals. Making a connection on LinkedIn is a way to start to build a connection with these professionals. Once they begin to trust your business and vice versa, they can start recommending you to their prospective clients. This type of word of mouth is a powerful tool to tap into.

Also, keep an open mind and remember that networking with the competition can sometimes be a good thing. If you have good working relationships with other businesses in your industry, you might get some free marketing. For example, if you have a construction business, it would be worth your while to be on good terms with some of the other businesses in your area. If another business is booked solid with no time to take on another job, they could refer the prospective client your way. They won't be willing to put their own reputation on the line and refer their potential clients to a total stranger. This is why it is important to have a connection with them, and LinkedIn is a great way to do that.

Tips and Tricks for Using LinkedIn for Your Business

- **Tap into your existing contacts.** Invite the people you already do business with to connect with you on LinkedIn. It will help boost your credibility to other professionals and businesses.

- **Reach out and make new connections.** Introduce yourself to other professionals and potential clients just like you would in a professional meeting.

- **Completely fill out your profile.** People are always skeptical of a profile that seems incomplete or lacking. Fill out as much information as you can, and always link back to your website.

- **Optimize your profile for searching on the web.** People won't be able to find your profile if you do not do this. Use important keywords that include your business location, key services, and industry buzz words.

- **Last but not least, keep it professional.** LinkedIn is not the place to share the crazy story of what happened at the bar. If you feel the need to share, do so on another social media platform.

How to Market Your Business Online Using Twitter

Twitter is one of the fastest growing social media platforms. It's a unique type of social media, with short posts called "Tweets" that are just 140 characters or less in length. You might not think that Tweets are substantial enough to market your business, but when used properly they are an effective tool. Here are some tips on getting started with Twitter, as well as tips on how your business can use Twitter.

- Choose the right Twitter handle. Pick a name that matches the name of your business. This makes it easy for people to find you, and leaves no questions about whether or not your Twitter persona really represents your business.

- Keep it short and simple. The great thing about Twitter is that it forces you to think carefully about the wording of your posts. You only get 140 characters, so you have to make effective use of them. And because they are so short, they are easy for people to read with a quick glance.

- The key to success is getting that quick glance at your post to lead to something more. Use the Tweet to tease them, and make them interested in learning more. You could post a link back to your website, offering more information about a special offer or something relevant to your business. If you get them to your website, you could easily get them to make a purchase. Or at the very least, you know you got your information out there.

- The other thing you want your Twitter followers to do is to repost or "re-Tweet" your Tweets. Come up with something that is funny, witty, or otherwise entertaining and people will share away. Likewise, if you post a good deal or savings, people will want to give their friends a heads up. Those friends may then become a follower of your business on Twitter.

- You can use hashtags to get more people to see your posts. A hashtag has a keyword with a number symbol in front of it, like this: #hashtag. Using a hashtag helps to organize and categorize your posts and makes them easier to sort.

- Start building your Twitter account by getting a few loyal and interested followers. Keep them interested by posting informative and interesting content. Interact with other businesses and Twitter users by reposting things relevant to your business.

- Don't ignore your followers. If they post a Tweet about your business, respond to it. Give them information, thank them, or respond to their criticism even if it is something negative. This shows your customers that you care about what they think.

What sort of things can you post on the Twitter page for your business?

- Links to sales and special offers that are open only to your twitter followers.

- Links to positive articles about your business in the local media.

- Testimonials from your happy customers.

- Responses to your customers' Tweets.

- Witty or funny posts. Not every Tweet has to be directly related to your business or product.

How to Market Your Business Online Using Facebook

Facebook has become the most widely used social network on the internet today. If you are going to use social media to market your business, Facebook is a good place to start. After all, it has the largest user network of any social networking site currently in operation.

Having a presence on Facebook is a great way to start building brand recognition. This is important for any type of business. If your business is new, Facebook is a way to start getting the attention of potential customers or clients. However, even well established businesses can benefit from being on Facebook. It is a good way to expand your customer base, but it is also a great way to reach out to current customers. You can use Facebook to market directly to your target audience.

How to Begin Marketing Your Business on Facebook

- The first thing you should consider doing is making a Facebook page for your business. Just like a personal profile, this is a good chance to show what your business is all about. It should explain what your business is and what you do. You should provide as much background on your business as possible, including a link to the website, information about services provided, contact information, address, and store hours. A page full of information will be helpful to your customers, and it will encourage them to use your page.

- After you've got a Facebook page with the basic information, you still have many options to market your business. Remember that the page is just the beginning. It is your virtual storefront, but just like a real store, you cannot just build it and let it sit there. You've got to find ways to attract people back to your page again and again.

- Remember to update your page regularly, because people forget about pages that aren't regularly updated. Anytime your business has something new to offer, you should mention it on your Facebook page. You can also update your page by posting photos, videos, or even testimonials for customers. The key is to keep your page visible to your customers. You want to have your posts show up in their news feed, so they do not forget you are there. Just don't go overboard, because too many posts can annoy your following.

- Use your page to interact with customers, rather than simply providing them with information. Use polls, questions, and contests to get them to interact with you on your page. You could create a poll asking what their favorite product is. Or you could even ask a crazy, out of the blue question just to get their attention.

- Another important thing is to tease them a bit to get them interested in what you have to offer. Create a post about a "special deal" that will be unlocked if your status gets 500 likes. Or offer a special coupon or discount to people who like your page.

- Last but certainly not least, look into Facebook's paid advertising. You can create an ad that features what your business has to offer, while promoting your page at the same time. This is also a great way to get more "likes" to your page. Having a great Facebook page is the number one step to getting started in social media marketing. Use these basic tips to help build your page and start attracting the attention of your prospects and customers.

How to Market Your Business Online Using Google+

Google+ is a new addition to the social media scene. It currently has well over 100 million members to date. Google+ marketing is a relatively new concept, however it is fast becoming a big player in the online marketing world. This is a result of having a special brand value attached to it. Google in general as you probably already know is recognized throughout the world for its search engine prowess, Android operating system, Chrome web browser, Gmail, maps and YouTube. This synergy is helping to propel Google+ to the top of the list as a marketing option for entrepreneurs and business owners.

1) **Create a Profile** – Your first step once you have signed up should be to create your Google+ profile. You must choose and upload a profile picture that will reflect your personal or business identity. It helps your marketing's cause when you add relevant information about your business, and the products and services that you offer to your profile. When describing your product or services, make sure you highlight their benefits.

    You can also customize your profile URL from the default. Use the same ending for your URL as your Twitter username, if the URL is available. Otherwise pick something else that sticks to your overall brand, but remember to keep it simple and as short as possible. This makes it much easier to remember and share.

2) **Create a Google+ Business Page** – Google allows businesses to create their own pages but first you need to

have a personal profile on Google+. The way that you create a Google+ Business Page is by clicking on the "create a page tool". Once you have done this you can then choose a category for your business page. Your category choices are the following. Product or Brand, Local Business or Place, Arts, Entertainment or Sports Company, Institution or Organization or Other.

Another great thing about Google+ Business Pages is that you are allowed to create multiple pages for your business. You can decide to have one main page for your business and also smaller pages that specifically focus on a certain product, service or event.

3) **Send out invitations** – Once you are all set up, it's time to send out invitations to as many people as you can who are related to or interested in your business to interact and share in the Google + experience. Once people follow you on Google+ you can then add them to your "circle". Once they have become part of your "circle" they will also began to see your posts in their "stream"

4) **Sharing on Stream** - For intensive Google+ marketing, this is your place to start sharing and interacting with other Google+ users. Post news updates and important information about your company. Make sure your media stream stays clean and devoid of anything improper or offensive.

You must also remember that people often subscribe to the credo "seeing is believing", so it is a good idea to put a nice collection of videos and photos about your business on your Google+ profile. A great album that captures all facets of your business could work wonders for the reputation of your company.

5) **The Google+ Badge** – There are two Google+ badges, one for pages and one for your profile. Google+ badges that link directly to your profile allow people to find you very easily on Google+ without missing a beat and add you to a circle directly from your website. Badges that link to the Google+ pages that you've created also have those same features as well as some additional functionality.

6) **Direct Connect** – Google has a feature called Direct Connect which makes it simple for users to find and follow brands on Google+ via Google Search. For example, if a user wanted to follow my company Make Profits Easy they would simply type in "+Make Profits Easy" in the Google Search box. This will bring up a direct link to the Make Profits Easy page.

How to Market Your Business Online Using Foursquare

What is Foursquare? Foursquare is a location based social network application that let consumers "check in" to locations and access free rewards or deals. Users can also share their location with family and friends when they have "checked in" via a smart phone app or by text message. Points are awarded to users when they've checked in to the various venues. When a user has accumulated the most points for checking in to a specific venue they are awarded with the distinct title of "Mayor" until someone passes their total points.

Foursquare has over 20 million users so there are many opportunities that exist to gain new customers for your business. In fact, here are some tips that illustrate how you can effectively market your business using Foursquare.

- **Set up your campaign** – The first thing you have to do is register with Foursquare. You do this by visiting www.foursquare.com and entering in your registration details. Once you have registered, you can create a page which allows you to reach consumers. Pages are easy to build and similar to Twitter, your fans can "follow" your page.

- **Start running specials** – Once you have set up your campaign start running specials. Your specials could include giving out exclusive discounts, gift cards or free merchandise to whoever gets crowned Mayor. This is a great way to acquire customers and get them in your store.

- **Get the word out** – Start letting your customers and prospects know about the specials that you have on Foursquare and they will spread the word to their family and friends. You can also promote your specials through other social media platforms such as Facebook, Google+ and Twitter.

- **Utilize the "to do list"** – Foursquare allows you to create a "to do list" for your followers. This can be beneficial to your business in the following way. You can use your "to do list" to show your customers some of your up and coming plans for improving your products and services or whatever else you think they might get excited about.

- **Track your results** – Foursquare has a built in functionality in the business dashboard that you have access to as an owner and operator of a venue that allows you to track and measure the results of your campaigns. You can track the customers or prospects that "check in" daily, weekly or monthly, that way you can see what's working and what's not and adjust your marketing strategy accordingly.

If appropriate for your business and I don't see why it wouldn't be, I highly recommend utilizing Foursquare as a marketing medium. It is free advertising for your business and automatically opens your business to hundreds, thousands or potentially millions of users. In addition, Foursquare allows you to strengthen the connection with your current customers by thanking and rewarding them for their business. This helps to build loyalty to your brand.

How to Market Your Business Online Using Pinterest

Pinterest is another one of those new additions to the big name players in social media. For being relatively new to the scene, Pinterest has seen monumental growth in a short period of time. While the site is predominantly used by women, there are several ways you can use it to market your business online.

Pinterest allows its users to visually share, and discover new interests by posting, also known as "pinning" images or videos to their own or others pinboards. This allows visitors to discover new things about topics that they may be interested in, or discover topics they know little about.

To become a member of Pinterest you must be invited by another member. However, don't fret if you don't know any Pinterest members that could send you an invitation, you can simply request an invitation by visiting www.pinterest.com and clicking on "Request an Invite" and entering your email address to be notified when you have access to create your account.

So how would you market your business on Pinterest? Like anything else it all starts with a plan.

- **Plan for success** – Once you have joined Pinterest and have set up your account you want to make sure that you have branded it with your logo. You also want to create a pin board that appeals to your target audience or the niche that you are trying to reach. You can accomplish this by pinning things that reflect the products or services that you have to offer.

- **Be strategic** – Of course you want to pin your own stuff, but it also important that you repin things that other people post so that you can build up a loyal tribe that will also share your pins with others. Remember that when other members repin the stuff that you post, they link directly back to your website which will result in a significant increase in traffic.

- **Be active** – Like any other social media site to see positive results you must be active on Pinterest. Comment or like other pins and tag other pinners as mentioned before this will allow you to build a loyal tribe that will reciprocate with sharing your pins.

- **Pin great content** – Pinterest is all about aesthetics so make sure that the content that you pin is visually appealing as well as interesting, because if you manage to accomplish both your pins have a great chance of going viral.

- **Utilize keywords and hashtags** - Just like on all other social sites, you should make effective use of keywords and hashtags related to your business and specifically to your products or services. Also, you can include links to your website in the description field for each pin you submit to the site, driving traffic and increasing visibility.

- **Utilize Your Tools** - Don't forget about the essential tool "Pin It" button, which is right on your browser once installed. Download the Pinterest app on your mobile devices so it can be accessed anywhere at any time.

- **Monitor and Measure Your Traffic** -By doing so, you will be able to find out what works and what doesn't, so you can focus more on the things that work. Also take a look at what your competitors and other businesses are doing. You might be surprised by what you could learn.

How to Market Your Business Online Using YouTube

One of the hottest trends in online marketing today is a plethora of businesses utilizing videos on YouTube to promote their products and services and show their expertise. Video allows businesses to create and share remarkable and engaging content with their audience in a way that plain text will never match.

Let's face it most people love videos because it allows them to connect visually and aurally in a fun way to the subject matter as opposed to arduously pouring over some boring text that consist of lengthy product descriptions. Tell me which one would you prefer?

YouTube is the social media site that is leading the video revolution. Owned by Google, YouTube now attracts over 800 million unique viewers per month so you can clearly see why this is the preferred destination for most businesses when they want to create and share their content with the world.

Here are some useful tips on how you can you use videos and YouTube to market your business to your targeted niche:

Take Every Opportunity to Make a Video

Create tutorial videos, general training videos and how-to videos. They can benefit the customers that you have already and turn your prospects into future customers, while increasing the exposure of your business. Make funny behind the scene videos. You can show a personal side to attract customers and further expose your brand. If you plan to launch a new line of products or host a significant event, you can consider developing a video blog. You may also want to make a video just to give an overview of your company or the service that you offer. No matter what video you are making, always try to be creative to keep your audience interested, engaged, and wanting to see more.

Create a Channel

Create a YouTube Channel for your business. This allows YouTube users to subscribe to your channel, and permits you to send out emails to the ones who subscribed to you. Link your videos to Facebook, Twitter, Google+, and any other websites that could increase exposure.

Maintain a Philosophy for Brand Recognition

Make sure to include the logo of your business at the beginning or end of your videos and make sure you also include a link back to your website in the description area. Establish a personality or "voice" for your videos. Make sure that it matches your branded tone which you have established through other marketing channels. Take every chance you can to let your videos stand out. Building your brand is just as important as selling your products.

Keywords are important

Make sure you utilize your main keywords in your video's description, title and tag section. Keywords allow your targeted users to reach you by typing relevant keywords into the YouTube search engine. It also enables the major search engines like Google, Yahoo and Bing to include your video in their search results.

Exploring the YouTube Community

Since YouTube is a social networking site you should find ways to establish your business within the YouTube community. Comment on other people's videos that are within your field of interest and this may inspire them to visit your channel, view your videos and also leave comments.

Embed your videos on your website

YouTube allows you to embed videos on your website via HTML code. You should use this feature to put your YouTube hosted videos on your site so that your website's visitors can also view your videos. Embedding your YouTube videos on your site instead of personally hosting them, saves on bandwidth and results in a faster download for your website's visitors.

How to Market Your Business Online Using Groupon

What is Groupon and how can you use it to market your business? Groupon is a deal-of-the-day social website that features coupon offers by local businesses to Groupon members. So for example, if you were a consumer from New York City and you signed up as a member on Groupon, you will receive daily email offers that consists of discounts that have been made available by businesses in your local area through the Groupon site.

The way that Groupon conducts business with the merchant is as follows. Groupon collects the money from the customers who have purchased the special offer. Groupon gives them the voucher/code that they need in order to redeem the offer. Groupon then takes 50% of the total revenue then gives the merchant the rest.

I know that you are probably wondering how does the merchant actually make money with a Groupon promotion when Groupon takes 50% of the proceeds and the merchant is also giving a huge discount to their customers that normally ranges anywhere from 50% to 90 % off?

Well in a lot of cases merchants do make money when they plan their promotion with an end goal in mind. That end goal could be to get new customers through the doors whom will ultimately make repeated purchases over time or the end goal could be to entice customers to come through the doors so that you can sell them an item on the back end with a bigger profit margin.

So basically you should have an end goal in mind, because a coupon is essentially a loss leader and with a loss leader you will almost certainly lose money on the discounted items, but the hope is that the customer will also spend money on other items, or even better, become a regular customer.

Before you make the decision to do a Groupon promotion for your business you should consider the following:

Your profit margin – As mentioned previously when you offer coupons they are essentially a loss leader, the chances that you are going to make money from the actual special offer are slim, so you have to structure your promotion in a way that allows you to make money, even if it's on the back-end. You also have to take into account that your business as a result of a Groupon promotion will instantly expose your business and brand to a wider audience.

Your inventory and the amount of space you have - A Groupon special offer normally leads to a huge influx of customers, so you have to make sure that you have a sufficient amount inventory to meet the demand and you have enough space at your place of business to accommodate all the customers that you will receive. If you don't properly plan for this, the results can be disastrous and you want to avoid that. You want your Groupon promotion to run as smoothly as possible.

Can you handle the influx of traffic? – When you do a Groupon promotion your website will be bombarded with traffic as a result of people trying to find out more about your business and location. Make sure that you have the bandwidth to handle all of the traffic, because you don't want your website crashing in the middle of your promotion. That will not be good for your business. In addition to increased website traffic, you will also be receiving numerous calls to your business, so make sure you have an adequate amount of phone lines available and the people to answer them.

Your cash flow – Groupon takes 50% of the proceeds of your special offer promotion and it takes some time for them to pay you, plus they may even pay you in installments, so you have to make sure that you are not dependent on receiving the money that you earned immediately and that it doesn't impact your daily cash flow operations.

How to Market Your Business Online Using Press Releases

Originally, press releases were designed to be a communication tool between a PR firm or company's PR staff and the media. These days, online news sites like Google News and Yahoo News include such an abundance of press releases making it easy to syndicate news, which has substantially upgraded the role of press releases as a marketing medium. Since press releases are now used as an effective tool to distribute content to consumers through media, they create an excellent opportunity for you to get your business out in front of the masses. Press releases are also a great opportunity for you to get incoming links or backlinks to your website which aids in your ranking in the major search engines.

When using progressive wire services such as PR Newswire, PRWeb, Market Wire and Business Wire, the process of getting your news content into the popular news search engines has been simplified. Of all the online news sites, including CNN, the New York Times, MSNBC, etc., Yahoo! News is the No. 1 destination for online news.

Realizing the great opportunity that press releases offer, a lot of businesses are using strategies to ensure that their press releases receive maximum exposure. If you have never written a press release before, then you need to become familiar with the standards and format expected of a press release. You may want to spend some time researching how press release writing is done before diving in, but here are some general instructions:

1) **Write a killer headline.** Since most people skim through headlines searching for things that jump out at them, your headline is one of the most important parts of the entire press release. You need to focus on getting people's attention with your headline. Reporters and other individuals in the media are not easily impressed, making it especially difficult to get them interested. You need to be unique and different, and you must stand out from the crowd. Even if you are writing about something that many consider boring, you must get creative and find a way to make it sound worth reading or learning more about. As for formatting, the headline should always be written in title case.

2) **Back it up with a strong sub-headline to add more details**. Take this as an opportunity to follow up with some extra information, but stick to keeping it interesting. The goal of the headline and sub headline is to reel the reader in so that

they read the rest of your press release.

3) **Answer the basic questions in the lead.** The next part of your press release is the lead, which typically addresses all the particular details of your story. Tell who the story is about, what they have done, where they are located and other information.

4) **Tell the story using the body of your press release.** This is where you want to include all the most important info related to your story. The body usually includes 2-4 short paragraphs and normally includes a quote somewhere within it from a key person involved in the news story (in this case, probably you!)

5) **Last comes the boilerplate, similar to a byline.** The boilerplate is the last part of your press release. It's sort of an "about us" section that is typically four to five sentences long.

6) **A final note on formatting.** At the end of your press release, you should always add the number symbol three times in a row with no spaces on a separate line. This is standard formatting for press releases and helps them to determine the end of your story. It would look like this ###, but it would be on its own line.

Of course, if you're not feeling confident enough to write your own press release, there are tons of services that will gladly write one for you in exchange for a fee. In fact, many press release distribution sites also offer writing services if you have the budget and aren't sure you can write one on your own.

Distributing Your Press Release to the Media

There are tons of sites online where you can submit your press release, some paid and others free. To maximize your results, you should probably submit to as many free ones as you can and also consider investing in a paid service to distribute them.

There is nothing wrong with free press release submission sites, and I have included a long list of them for you to submit to in this section. Some of the sites listed are also paid services, such as PRWeb.

The advantage to using a paid service is that the company will send your press release to thousands of media contacts that the company has worked to develop. More journalists and reporters will see your news story this way, and they will take it more seriously because they trust the company you have paid to handle distribution.

Most paid press release sites (and even some of the free ones) manually review each and every press release they receive before they approve it and send it out. A paid service basically guarantees that your press release gets tons more visibility and it can be a great way to attract interested radio show producers looking for interviews and many other people who would like to offer an opportunity to share your expertise.

List of Press Release Submission Sites

1. PR Web (http://www.prweb.com)
2. PR Log (http://www.prlog.org)
3. eReleases (http://www.ereleases.com)
4. PR News Lead (http://www.prnewslead.com)
5. Online PR News (http://www.onlineprnews.com)
6. Press Release 365 (http://www.pressrelease365.com)
7. Express Press Release Distribution (http://express-press-release.net)

8. 24-7 Press Release (http://www.24-7pressrelease.com)
9. PR Newswire (http://www.prnewswire.com)
10. WebWire (http://www.webwire.com)
11. iNewswire (http://www.inewswire.com)
12. Marketwire (http://www.marketwire.com)
13. PR Leap (http://www.prleap.com)
14. PressWire (http://www.presswire.com)
15. PR Buzz (http://www.prbuzz.com)
16. My PR Genie (http://www.myprgenie.com)
17. Real Wire (http://www.realwire.com)
18. PR Nine (http://www.prnine.com)
19. Press King (http://www.pressking.com)
20. PR Free (http://www.prfree.com)
21. PR Zoom (http://www.przoom.com
22. Press Release Circle (http://www.pressreleasecircle.com)
23. Press Release Sender (http://www.pressreleasesender.com)
24. Source Wire (http://www.sourcewire.com)
25. Blurb Point (http://www.blurbpoint.co.uk)
26. Free Press Release Center (http://www.freepressreleasecenter.com)
27. Press Method (http://www.pressmethod.com)
28. Press Release Point (http://www.pressreleasepoint.com)
29. Free Press Index (http://www.freepressindex.com)
30. Submit Free PR (http://www.submitfreepr.com)
31. 1888PressRelease (http://www.1888pressrelease.com
32. Wide PR (http://www.widepr.com)
33. PR Blue (http://www.prblue.com)

34. Release Wire (http://www.releasewire.org)
35. Send 2 Press (http://www.send2press.com)
36. PR Underground (http://www.prunderground.com)
37. eWorld Wire (http://www.eworldwire.com)
38. Online PR News (http://www.onlineprnews.com)
39. EZ PR (http://www.ezpr.org)
40. Submit Press Release 123 (http://www.submitpressrelease123.com)

How to Market Your Business Online Using Ebooks

Just in case you didn't know an ebook is an electronic version of a book. Depending on the format it can be read on a computer or an *ebook* reader. Some of the most popular ebook readers include Amazon's Kindle, Barnes and Noble's Nook, and the Sony e-reader just to name a few.

Ebooks are a great and convenient way to get your core message out to your target audience. They are also an easy way for you to establish credibility by providing valuable content to your prospects and customers. Ebook marketing has been around since the inception and the explosion of the internet and it is the go to choice for savvy internet marketers who are looking to quickly build their subscriber list.

The "Free Report" Ebook

If you are looking to build up your email subscriber list fast and get prospects into your sales funnel, the best way to do it is by giving away a free report in the form of a pdf ebook. Your ebook doesn't have to be the size of a novel in terms of pages, but in order for it to be effective it must deliver value to its intended recipients.

For example, as a creative real estate investor, I am primarily trying to find sellers who are motivated to sell their property. One way that I market to find these particular motivated sellers is by placing a classified ad in the local newspaper that basically states that I am looking to buy houses creatively. In order to get them to respond to my particular ad, as an enticement I offer them a free report in the ebook format entitled "How To Sell Your Home In 7 days" that they can download online by visiting my website http://dependablehomebuyers.com.

This informative ebook is only 14 pages in length, but it provides valuable and useful information that illustrates to the motivated seller the various creative ways in which I can buy their house. It also explains to them step by step how they can sell their house within 7 days. This particular ebook report also contains a "call to action" that instructs them to either fill out a form on my website for further follow-up or they can personally call me so that I can assess their situation and offer a possible solution to their real estate dilemma. This ebook marketing approach has worked wonders for my real estate business.

Let's face it, people love the word "free" and by offering them an informative ebook for free this gives you permission to market to them. They know who you are and expect to hear from you because they have "raised their hand" and indicated that they are interested in what you have to offer.

You can also create an ebook and offer it for free with the intention of making a back-end sale. For example, I have also authored a real estate home study course entitled "The Real Estate Investors Guide to Finding Motivated Sellers" where I teach other aspiring real estate entrepreneurs how to attract and find motivated sellers. It's a proprietary system and it is priced at $497. I know that a lot of people are gun-shy when it comes to purchasing something at a certain price point because for the most part they are skeptical and that's understandable.

The way that I erase their skepticism is by offering a free report. The free report that I offer is entitled "Finding The Motivated Seller: The Key To Your Success As a Real Estate Entrepreneur" and it's available at http://www.findingthemotivatedsellers.com. Once they have read this report they develop more confidence which will lead a great deal of them to purchasing the full-blown home study course priced at $497.

Paid Ebook

You don't necessarily have to give an ebook away for free to reach your target audience and gain customers. You can also sell the ebook that you have created. You can sell it in the form of a pdf on your website or you can sell it as a kindle or nook book on Amazon or Barnes and Noble respectively. I prefer to sell my ebooks on Amazon.com because they have a wider reach and have 80% of the market in terms of ebook sales. They also have an incredible platform for ebook selling called Kindle Direct Publishing where they pay a 35%-70% royalty rate for each ebook that you sell.

In addition, when you enroll your ebook exclusively in their Kindle Select Program they allow you to give away your ebook for free for 5 days out of a 90 day period. What does this mean to you as a marketer? It gives you access to a worldwide audience. Presently, Amazon allows you to sell ebooks in the following countries: Germany, United Kingdom, Italy, India, Japan and France. From my personal experience, kindle owners are voracious readers and when you offer something for free, they will download it and give it a try.

My best free download result to date was 4,000 plus downloads for my kindle ebook entitled "How to Start An Online Business with Less Than $200". Can you imagine? 4,000 potential prospects! After the 5 day free download period was over I immediately experienced a bump in sales because I was now part of Amazon's ecosystem. More importantly, I was able to pick up a few new clients on the back-end.

Selling kindle ebooks on Amazon has become such an integral part of my ebook marketing strategy that I have become adept at marketing my books. I really have discovered the secrets to promoting them and if you want to also learn the exact methods that I use I have made them available in my kindle ebook entitled "How to Promote Market and Sell Your Kindle Book".

How to Market Your Business Online Using Email Marketing

When done right email marketing can be an effective way for you to develop and build a relationship with your customers or prospective clients. I say "done right" because email marketing has lost some of its luster do to the rampant abuse of spam. As a result of being bombarded with spam people have become sort of desensitized when they receive email in their inbox because they don't know whether it's legitimate or junk.

In fact, when I first began utilizing email marketing in 2004, I experienced nearly an 80% open rate for every email offer or correspondence that I sent out. This phenomenal open rate was to due to fact that having an email address was a fairly new concept and people just couldn't wait to log into their email account to see who sent them email.

Boy times sure have changed. Now people have multiple email addresses where is back then they mainly had only one. They now have an email address that they use for family and friends and then they may have an email address or two strictly for the things that they signed up for online. The emails that arrive from family and friends of course gets opened, but the other email inbox that they use to sign up for the things online rarely gets opened.

So your goal first and foremost with email marketing is to get your emails opened, because if they don't your message will never be read. The following is some of the things that you can do to ensure that you have a high open email rate.

The From Field

People usually scan through their email inbox and immediately look at the "from" list and the subject line. If they do not recognize who it is from, they either delete the email or don't open it at all. The same goes for the subject line especially if it doesn't interest them. So before deciding to send them email make sure they recognize where it's from. This will be primarily based on the previous interaction you had with them. For example, if they are familiar with your business's name then you want to make sure that when you send them your email that it is from your business email address so that way they will recognize it as soon as they see it in their "from" list in their email inbox.

The Subject Line

Your subject line must be interesting or your emails will not get open. Also your subject line should describe the content of the email. There shouldn't be anything deceptive about it and you want to make sure that it is not spammy looking, so you want to avoid words like "free", "make money" and phrases like "once in a lifetime opportunity" because your email won't get through or pass the spam filters.

The Timing

The time that you send out your email is a very important factor in getting it opened. You don't want to send out an email too early in the morning or too late in the night. You want to perform various tests to determine the best time to send out your emails, by doing so this will help to improve your open rates.

Personalization

You want to make sure that you personalize the emails that you send out by using the person's first name in the email itself and perhaps in the subject line. This will help to increase your open rate as much as 10% because you are capturing your reader's attention by making your email unique to them.

How to Market Your Business Online Using Ezine Advertising

What's an ezine? It's an electronic newsletter or magazine. Ezines are delivered to subscribers by email or they are simply made available online. I have advertised in ezines over the years with a great deal of success mainly because ezine advertising is highly targeted. For example, you can specifically advertise in ezines that are in your particular niche. If you sell golf products, there are ezines that are available that cater solely to golfers. If you are in the healthy living niche there are ezines that cater to health related issues and have subscribers who follow and read them.

Other benefits to ezine advertising are:

- They are one of the fastest ways to get traffic to your site
- The readers are very responsive
- It's inexpensive
- It's easy to test and track results

However, it is imperative that you do your due diligence before you begin your marketing campaign via ezines. Here are some of the things that you should take into account.

- **The ezine's niche** – You want to make sure that you advertise in ezines that reach your target audience or your marketing won't be effective. So the key to successful ezine advertising is to find ezines that are in the same category as the product or service that you sell. This will not only ensure that you reach your targeted audience but it will also ensure that when they discover your ad they are more likely to read it because it caters to the topic or subject that they are interested in.

- **The ezine's amount of subscribers** – You want to know how many subscribers an ezine has before advertising, because you want to get the most bang for your buck. Some of the smaller ezines (less than 15,000) have to charge more for advertising or they will simply go out of business. While the medium (20,000 – 80,000) and larger size ezines (80,000 and up) don't have to do that and they actually cost less per thousand readers. Another advantage of advertising in medium and large size ezines is that they usually archive their issues on their website which gives you increased advertising exposure over time.

- **Make sure that your ad is well written** – An ad that is well written can generate a huge response, while a poorly written one will have the opposite effect. So make sure that your ad is well written and it stands out. The job of your ad should be to sell the click, not really the product or service. When you sell the click, the click can lead them back to your website and a sign up form via your autoresponder which will allow you to capture their information and do a series of follow-ups that will hopefully lead to a sale.

There are mainly 3 different ezine advertising formats that are available to you as a marketer, here are those ad formats:

Classified ads – Based on my personal experience classified ezine advertising is the least effective because they are grouped with so many other classified ads that are also vying for the same attention. Most ezines offer free classified advertising when you sign up as a subscriber.

Sponsor ads – Sponsorship ads are way more responsive than classified ads so they cost more. An ezine normally has 2 to 3 sponsor ads per issue and they are usually located at the top of the issue for higher visibility.

Solo ads – These are stand alone ads that an ezine sends out separately from its issue to their subscribers. Solo ads get the most exposure, so therefore they are more expensive than sponsor and classified ads. Solo ads also allow you tell more of your story in a sales letter fashion.

Now that you know how beneficial ezine advertising can be for your business and you are aware of the advertising formats, where exactly would you find ezines that cater to your particular niche? There are many resources out there that have this information but the best and most reliable source for finding out that information is Charlie Page's Directory of Ezines located at the following web address http://www.directoryofezines.com.

How to Market Your Business Online Using Blogs

So what exactly is a blog and what is blogging? How can a blog and blogging assist you with connecting with your target audience and enable you to grow your business? Well for starters a blog is simply a journal that is available only online. The activity of updating a blog is called "blogging" and someone who keeps and maintains a blog is called a "blogger."

A blog is a great complement to your website and a blog helps to personalize your business and the products and services that you have to offer by opening up a direct communication channel with your prospects and customers. This direct communication with your prospects and customers keep them engaged with the activities of your business.

Other benefits of having a blog for your business are the following:

- It helps you differentiate your business and your products and services from others.
- It embeds your brand's identity into the consciousness of your audience.
- It allows you to position yourself as the expert.
- It serves as the perfect lead generation tool.
- It enables you to demonstrate and communicate how your products and services solve your customer's problems.

Now that you know what the benefits of having a business blog are there are some key decisions you need to make before you create one. Some of the decisions you have to make include the following:

1) **What do you want to accomplish with your blog?** You must determine what your specific goals are. Are you using it as a lead generation tool, customer service tool or a research and development tool? Are you strictly using it for branding purposes or to promote a product or a service?

2) **What target audience are you trying to reach?** The target audience you are trying to attract will determine the composition of your blog in terms of content. The content

must match and appeal to the audience you are trying to reach.

3) **Who will be in charge of the blogging and how often will they make posts?** To build a loyal following for your blog, there must be frequent and consistent posts or your blog readers will lose patience and interest. If you are a one person operation or you don't have the time to make posts, you can just outsource the task.

4) **What blog software or platform will you choose?** There are many blog software or platforms available and you have to choose the one which works best with your business. Here are some of the more popular blog platforms that exist in the marketplace today.

Wordpress – Wordpress is the most popular blog platform used today. It is free and easy to install and has countless plugins available. Blogs that run on the Wordpress platform can be hosted at WordPress.com, or the WordPress software can be downloaded and can be hosted on your own server or a third party server.

TypePad – Is a paid blog hosting service that has thousands of professional designs for you to use. Depending on the TypePad package you buy, you'll have a different amount of features available to you. TypePad is great for people who are new to blogging. Typepad blogs are hosted by Typepad, so if you decide to choose them remember that your blog will have a ".typepad.com" extension after the blog's domain name.

Movable Type – Just like Wordpress is also free and open source however, they also offer a paid version for businesses who are looking for more blog flexibility. The Movable Type platform powers more than just blogs and it is a fully-functional web site and content management system.

Blogger – Blogger.com is Google's free blogging service and you are given your own subdomain. The main drawback with Blogger is that blogs created with Blogger.com display a bar at the top of the page with the Blogger logo and links to other blogs so there is little chance for branding with your logo.

Tumblr - Tumblr is a free micro-blogging platform that has a simple and intuitive interface. It has many themes to choose from and it is easy for you to post photos, text, videos and slideshows. You are also able to choose a custom domain.

Guest Blogging

In addition to having your own business blog, you can also reach your target audience and expand your marketing's reach by guest blogging. Guest blogging is when you write posts to be published on other people's blogs. There are numerous benefits to guess blogging and here are a few of them:

- **It exposes you to a new and wider audience** – You get instant exposure to a new and wider audience which is simply awesome .People who may have never heard of you or your business before are now being exposed to you as a result of your posts being published on a blog other than your own.

- **You get a link back to your site** – When you guess blog on another site at the beginning of your post, or right after the end of your post there is a brief description of who you are, your specialty, and there is also a link included that leads back to your website. This results in increased traffic for your site and possible new customers.

- **You are recognize as an expert** – When you provide valuable information and content in your post as a guess blogger, you are seen as an expert on the subject matter. This instills confidence and trust in your audience and when they have a problem in the particular area or topic that you've discussed in your post they will seek you out and this will result in new business and new clients for you.

- **Relevant and high quality backlinks** – Relevant backlinks from blogs in your niche will do wonders for your search rankings in the major search engines. The search engines will view your website as a quality and authority site, because it has other quality sites linking back to it.

There are certain things that you should consider before agreeing to guest blog on other sites and the following represents a list of them.

Check out a site's traffic and influence. I know it sounds cool that someone asked you to guest blog on their site, but before agreeing to do so, you want check out the amount of traffic that they receive at their site. You can do this by going to Alexa.com and typing their web address in the search bar and it will render those numbers.

You also want to measure a site's influence. You can do this by checking out their social media profiles on sites like Twitter and Facebook. On Twitter you can check to see how many followers they have and on Facebook you can check out how many "likes" they have on their page or how many fans that they have in general. This will help you determine if it is worth your while to guess blog on their site.

Make sure that they are in the niche you are trying to target – You want to make sure that the site you are considering to guess blog on has the targeted audience you are trying to reach or you will be wasting your marketing efforts. So it is essential that you research or inquire about the demographics and the psychographics of their audience.

Make sure that they allow a link back to your site – Don't just assume that the site you are considering to guess blog on will link back to your site. It is best to make sure first, so there are no misunderstandings. The whole purpose of guess blogging is to reach a wider audience and gain additional traffic back to your site and if a site doesn't allow a link back to your site, what would be the purpose of guess blogging for them?

How to Market Your Business Online Using Webinars

The word "webinar" is the amalgamation of "web and "seminar". A "webinar" is a web-based seminar, a lecture, workshop, or presentation transmitted online. Most of the time webinars are usually live and they incorporate audio and visual elements as well as attendee interaction. More and more businesses have discovered the advantages that webinars have to offer and have started offering them in addition to or instead of more traditional face-to-face seminars.

What makes webinars so attractive to business owners are their flexibility, affordability, efficiency and effectiveness. Another advantage is that participants don't have to travel in order to attend. They can listen and watch a webinar from the comforts of their office or home. You also have the ability to digitally record your webinar presentation for future playback. This allows you to reach a much larger audience over a longer period of time.

Webinars also enables businesses to cut down on traveling and other expenses that they would normally incur with more traditional seminars and conferences. So basically, all you need to host your own webinar is a computer, internet access and a phone line.

There are various formats that you can use to plan a webinar for your business. Here are a few examples.

- **A Training Session.** This webinar format is ideally suited for transferring skills and knowledge. You can use this format to show your customers how to use your products or services or you can use it to educate and train your affiliates.

- **A Keynote Presentation.** With this particular format you will be doing most of the talking, and after you have finished, you can have a Q & A session with your attendees or sell them a product right on the spot. All you would have to simply do is put a "Buy it Now" or "Add to Cart" button right on the webinar's presentation page. This strategy for selling a product is very effective and it results in impulse purchases.

- **Interviewing an Expert.** With this format you are interviewing an expert for your audience. The interviewing an expert format is great for when you have a financial stake in a joint venture partnership with an expert in your field or another industry.

- **Coaching or Mentoring.** Webinars normally are group sessions however, you can use them to do one on one coaching or mentoring with your clients. If you have a consultant business this type of format would be ideal for you.

Now that you know some of the webinar formats that are available, here are some examples of what a webinar can do for your business:

Introduce your business or brand

A webinar can introduce your business and you personally to the public. Hosting and conducting a webinar allows you to represent your business and give it a face by associating a personality to it.

This gives assurances to your audience that your business is in fact a real live and breathing entity.

Become a recognized authority

A webinar is a great way to show your expertise and build your reputation. It can also enable you to be known as a "Guru" or a recognized authority in your particular niche.

Promote products

Webinars can be used to promote a product or service. What better way is there to sell a product or service but to a live, engaged and attentive, audience online? Generally, the way a product is promoted through a webinar is a speaker will discuss a topic with their audience and then refer to a particular product or service that will help their audience further grasp the subject matter like a home study course or coaching.

Increase sales

It is a known fact that webinars result in increased sales for a business because they help attendees understand better the benefits that will be derived from a particular product or service

Communicate with customers on a more personal level

Webinars allow business owners to keep in touch and stay connected with their customers. Businesses can harness the technology used for this method to personalize their services. Whether a webinar is offered for free or as a paid service, they are always very effective as a means to interact with your target audience.

It is easy to set up and run a webinar, the following below is an outline of the steps that you should follow.

Steps of Setting up and Running a Webinar

1. **Platform**. Many different services are available out there can help you successfully run a webinar. Both free ones like AnyMeeting and paid services such as GoToWebinars are your options to choose from. You must do your due diligence and research the various platforms before making a choice. Some service providers are great for hosting smaller events while others are great for much larger meetings. You will find a wide variety of special features, functions and offers when comparing service providers.

2. **Equipment**. Almost all the desktops and laptops can easily run any of the seminar software provided by your service provider. This bodes well for you as well as your webinar attendees. Some of the things that you will need to host your webinar include a recording, a bridge line, a transcript, an outline, an autoresponder, and a squeeze page.

3. **Content**. Most webinars include slide shows. A slideshow should act as an outline for both your audience and yourself. Keep the text on the slide show to a minimalistic, bullet point format. You can also throw in a little visual flare by adding images to the slides. The images can also consist of graphs or charts to support the points you are talking about.

4. **Email**. It is a smart idea to combine email marketing and webinars. Most of the webinar software has the function for you to send out email reminders before the time of the webinar. You can also use an autoresponder service such as Aweber to create a series of emails before and after the webinar.

How to Market Your Business Online Using Articles

Having a website is not enough to build a profitable business online. There are a great number of things that you need to consider in order for your online marketing to be effective, but the main component will always be TRAFFIC!

One of the best strategies to drive traffic to your website is article marketing; by adding a link back to your own website at the end of every article, you make it easier for readers to learn more about you, your products, and your overall business. Better yet, there are already numerous article directories where you can submit your articles and where search engines can find them easily. This translates into more traffic driven to your site simply because you are using that website's rank and reputation to boost your own.

There are quite a few online marketers that have built a steady fan (and customer) base through article marketing only! However, there are various things you should keep in mind.

Be Patient. Don't expect to attract thousands of readers with a single article –it simply doesn't work that way. It takes time for people to get to know you and your style; to create a buzz big enough to draw more readers through word-of-mouth. However, if you are consistent and proficient, all your efforts will be rewarded.

Do It Regularly. The secret to becoming a good writer is practice. So write, and then write some more! Also, the more you write, the more "regular" readers will be looking forward to your next article, and the faster they'll want to spread the word. If you don't like the idea of writing your own articles and submitting them manually to the thousands of article directories, you can outsource the task. My company Get Seo Backlinks (http://www.getseobacklinks.com) offers an SEO article writing and submission service in addition to SEO and premium link building that is primarily designed to get website owners to the top of the major search engines like Google, Yahoo and Bing for the main keywords that are relevant to their site.

Headlines Are Crucial! Your articles' headlines determine whether someone will read through the rest of your content or not. There are some "headline formulas" with which you can't go wrong such as: "X Ways to [insert goal here]" or the classic "How to [insert achievement here]". In general, anything that spikes readers' curiosity while staying on topic works!

Write Intuitively. Your content should lead readers from one paragraph to the next. The greatest thing about writing nowadays is you can proofread your article as many times as necessary to make sure it "reads well" before even saving it into your hard-drive.

Be Informative. Educate and let people see you as an expert and they will come back to learn more; help readers find a solution to their problems and they will start to follow you in unconscious gratitude.

Stir Emotions. Good copywriting is the kind of writing that can drive a reader to take action –whether it's signing up for a business newsletter or filling out a contact form. Take some time out of every week to study copywriting and learn how to stir people's emotions while channeling them through to your other marketing strategies.

Add a Personal Touch. Believe it or not, article marketing can actually help you connect with other people. The secret is educating and providing value while at the same time letting people relate to you by telling them about your own experiences and views.

How to Market Your Business Online by Creating an Affiliate Program

Imagine having half a dozen people promoting your business; now imagine having fifty people…or a hundred, or a thousand!

Affiliate marketing is one of the best ways to promote your business. Basically, affiliate marketing means paying a business partner (the affiliate) a commission whenever their efforts lead to a sale. In fact, you can reward a commission for some other action generated by the affiliate, it doesn't have to be just for generating a sale. Here are the other ways you can choose to reward your affiliates.

Pay per click – You can pay your affiliate a commission every time you receive a visitor to your website as a result of someone clicking on the affiliate's link.

Pay per lead - Pay per lead involves rewarding your affiliates a commission for generating leads for your business. Every time your affiliate gets a prospects' contact information they will get paid for doing so.

Pay per impression – You will pay your affiliate every time your ad is viewed by a visitor.

Cost per action (CPA) – You pay your affiliate based on a qualifying action such as a sale or a registration.

Large companies like Amazon.com phenomenal growth was due primarily to their affiliates and you can also grow your business quickly by having your own affiliate program.

You can also join an affiliate program and create an additional revenue stream for your business. To make it work successfully, all you would have to do is make sure that the products that you promote complement your business.

There are several things to consider when creating an affiliate program:

- **Stand out from the Rest.** You've probably seen dozens of affiliate programs, and so have the people you are trying to recruit, so you need to make sure you reach out to them properly so they'll pick YOU over any competitor.

- **The Right Tools.** You need a way to manage, track and pay your affiliates. Your affiliates need a way to view their statistics and have a way to access the promotional tools that you provide for them. There are many affiliate management software that can accomplish this task. The one that I presently use to manage, track and pay my affiliates is called Jrox.

- **Well-designed Websites.** People still respond best to visually attractive content. Make sure that your website and the website's of your affiliates are visually attractive.

- **Persuade with Words.** In addition to a visual appeal, make sure that your website as well as the marketing materials that you provide to your affiliates contains words that persuade and inspire people to purchase something or take a specific action that you intend. This will enable your affiliates to promote your business efficiently.

- **Offer Personalized Support.** Make sure you work together with your affiliates and provide great support. This includes educating them thoroughly about the products and services that you offer. You can schedule regular conference calls or webinars to answer questions collectively. This is also a great way for you to receive valuable input from your affiliates.

How to Market Your Business Online Using Sponsored Reviews

A sponsored review is an article written about your products, your company, or your services, which links readers to your website or blog in case they want to know more.

There are quite a few websites that connect bloggers and webmasters with advertisers looking to promote their businesses online. Basically, bloggers create an account and register their blogs into a huge database, and the advertiser (you) register to hire their services.

The cost depends on the website which links advertisers with bloggers. Most websites allow companies to bid in order to have a review written by a specific blogger; others allow the advertisers to contact the bloggers directly and buy a review from them at a listed price.

Sponsored reviews are mostly used when launching a company or website to increase exposure and spread the word! They are also an excellent way to build links –which in turn will help improve your website's ranking among search engines– and drive traffic to your website. However, there are a few things you should keep in mind:

1. **Do Your Homework**

    Take your time to do your research and choose a sponsored review website that meets your needs. Once you have chosen a website, take your time to choose a blogger (or bloggers) who will review your products or your website –don't look for the cheapest, but for the one who provides the best value.

2. **Find Relevant Blogs**

    Blogs that are successful and have a large following are blogs that focus on a specific theme or niche; a blog that's "all over the place" just isn't as appealing! Make sure you find blogs that relate to your products in order to drive targeted traffic to your website. Quite simply, the more targeted your traffic, the easier it is to make a sale!

3. **Look for Samples**

    When looking for bloggers and webmasters to write a sponsored review, take a good look at samples of their previous work. You want to find someone who'll write an honest review, without going out of their way to badmouth or over-praise.

4. **Ask for Help**
   If you have trouble figuring out how a sponsored review website works, or don't have the slightest idea of which blogs will target the right potential customers, ask for help. Professionals can help you come up with a proper strategy to implement sponsored reviews into your marketing efforts and make sure you're not just wasting your time and your hard-earned cash!

5. **Prepare for Criticism!**
   Webmasters who write sponsored reviews are not expected to write positive reviews all the time –not even because they're getting paid! However, this doesn't mean that an honest review won't drive traffic to your website. And as long as constructive criticism is provided, you'll be able to gather these sponsored reviews and –if a pattern is visible– use them to positively improve your business.

How to Market Your Business Online Using Pay Per Click Advertising

Pay per click advertising (PPC) is a great way to get targeted relevant traffic to your business website. It's also a great way to get instant visibility in the search engines. There are many pay per click advertising programs available on the internet. The most notable pay per click advertising program is Google Adwords. There is also the Microsoft Advertising Ad Center platform which incorporates both Bing and Yahoo search engines.

I don't want to jump the gun and assume that you know how pay per click advertising works so let me briefly explain it. Pay per click or PPC is a method for generating traffic wherein you pay for every visitor that goes to your website by clicking on your advertising link.

The cost that you pay per click is determined by the original bid that you placed on the particular keyword that resulted in your ad being shown in the search engines. So if you bid let's say 70 cents for the keyword "Healthy Living" and someone clicked on your ad it will cost you 70 cents or less depending on what others have bid for that exact keyword, your quality score and your click through rate when advertising on Google Adwords.

Pay per click advertising is a big part of my search engine domination strategy for my business. I use it mainly because it is effective, I am able to get immediate results and it represents 15% of all search engine traffic on the internet.

Here are some of the advantages of using pay per click advertising for your business:

- You get immediate results. Google Adwords ads become live in their search engine within 10 minutes of the ad being place.

- Your website receives targeted relevant traffic from the search engines as well as from partner websites that participate in the affiliate programs like Google Adsense.

- You only spend what your budget allows.

When investing in pay per click advertising you must use good economic common sense in determining whether it is working for you. The ultimate guideline for any pay per click advertising is how much business is it bringing you? If you're paying $100 per day in click fees to advertise cell phones, but you're only generating $75 per day in revenue from that ad then you either need to cut back on your advertising (lowering your per click bids) or improve your site's conversion rate from visitor to sale.

It's important not to get too attached to ads that don't work just because you think they should work. It may take as little as a week, or as long as three months to determine whether a particular pay per click ad is effective, but as long as you monitor your spending and your earnings closely and adjust your ads accordingly, you can generate positive income with paid search listings.

Here are some other things that you need to keep in mind when implementing pay per click advertising in your online marketing.

1. **Finding a PPC Provider.** There are many pay per click advertising programs available. So you have to make sure that you choose the ones that are suitable for your business.
2. **Start Small.** When venturing into the world of PPC advertising, start with a small budget (even if you can afford more). This will allow you to get a better understanding of how PPC works, and how it can benefit your business.
3. **Tweak 'til You Get It Right.** Make small modifications periodically and keep tracking your statistics to make the most out of every dollar you spend on PPC. You'd be surprised how the smallest changes can have the biggest impact in your advertising's effectiveness.
4. **Track and Measure Your Results.** Keeping a close eye on how your PPC advertising campaigns are performing is crucial to figuring out the best way to market your products and services. Measure your return on investment (roi) and if pay per click advertising is not making good economic sense for your business, then by all means eliminate it.

How to Market Your Business Online Using Online Classified Ads

Online classified ads are a great way to market your products and services online. There are virtually no restrictions regarding specific industries or niches; you could be located anywhere in the world; and anyone from individuals to large corporations has access to classified ads online.

There are several reasons why online classifieds are superior to regular, printed media classifieds including:

- **Lower Costs**
  Although costs vary, online classified ads are a very affordable marketing option. There are also free online classified ad sites.

- **Greater Reach**
  For a fraction of the cost of having a classified ad printed in your local newspaper, you can publish an online classified that reaches maybe three or four times as many people, AND without being limited to a specific area.

- **Easily Modified**
  It is obvious that having a printed classified is much more hassle than publishing one online just look at the materials and mechanisms necessary for any printing media. Also, some online classified websites allow their users to modify their ads at any moment.

Like any other marketing strategy, there are a few things you should keep in mind when creating an online classified ad:

Headlines

Your ad's headline is what makes the first impression on people. Unconsciously, people will decide whether it's worth spending the next few seconds reading the rest of the classified –or whether they should move on to something else– based solely on your headline.

Make sure your headline is appealing without being too "wordy" – try to sum up the main idea of your ad in 7 to 10 words; any more words and you'll risk losing them to the competition.

Keep It Simple

Every online classified ad website is different, and each has its own limits regarding the amount of characters (or words) allowed per advertisement. However, this is not the only reason why you should keep things short and simple; if you post a long ad to try and "cover all the basis", you'll probably end up boring readers, causing them to move on to the next ad before they're even done reading yours.

Stay Fresh

Online classified ads are usually displayed chronologically: newer postings are displayed first! So, when you've had a classified ad online for a couple of weeks, it's probably a good idea to make sure it hasn't been buried beneath hundreds of newer ads. People won't go through every single page on a classified ad website. They usually go through a few pages, and if they can't find what they're looking for, they move on to the next website. You need to do everything you can to ensure that your ad is among the first pages (if not the very first page).

To get you started on your online classified ad journey, the following is a list of free online classified ad websites that you can use to market your business.

1) http://www.Craigslist.com
2) http://www.kijiji.com
3) http://www.kwikposts.com
4) http://www.postlets.com
5) http://www.yahooclassifieds.com
6) http://www.salespider.com
7) http://www.myyja.com
8) http://www.zillow.com
9) http://www.betterbizlist.com
10) http://www.zikbay.com
11) http://www.kaboodle.com
12) http://www.kellywantads.com
13) http://www.sell.com
14) http://www.like123.com
15) http://www.ad4free.net
16) http://www.zamzata.com
17) http://www.findstuff.com
18) http://www.classifieds8.com
19) http://www.classifiedsforfree.com

20) http://www.marketingeasy.net

21) http://www.mcslist.com

22) http://www.ukulju.tripod.com

23) http://www.ozarksfirst.com

24) http://www.freeclassifieds100.com

25) http://www.bearzweb.com

26) http://www.freelinks.com

27) http://www.freebizadsweb.com

28) http://www.colemannews.com

29) http://www.dmoz.org

30) http://www.newfreeclassifiedads.com

31) http://www.myfreeclassifiedads.com

32) http://www.enamul.info/linkclassifieds.php

33) http://www.transworld-ads.com

34) http://www.Infotube.net

35) http://www.Classifiedsforfree.com

36) http://www.Olx.com

37) http://www.UsFreeAds.com

38) http://www.DomesticSale.com

39) http://www.Recycler.com

40) http://www.backpage.com

41) http://www.freeadscity.com

42) http://www.Adpost.com

43) http://www.Monkeyads.com

44) http://www.Tampaonlineclassifieds.com

45) http://www.oodle.com

46) http://www.buysellcommunity.com

47) http://www.webclassifieds.com

48) http://www.Domesticsale.com

49) http://www.Pennysaver.com

50) http://www.Owner.com

51) http://www.Tampa4sale.com

52) http://www.openrealtylist.com

53) http://www.rentomatic.com

54) http://www.homesalewizard.com

55) http://www.geebo.com

56) http://www.Ourclassifieds.org

57) http://www.Njville.com

58) http://www.USfreeads.com

How to Market Your Business Online by Using Ebay

Ebay is a great place to market and promote your business for these simple reasons:

- It has a built in marketplace consisting of 180 million register users who are predominantly buyers
- Selling items on Ebay requires little or no capital at all when you use the principles of leverage.
- There are over 18,000 categories for items.
- You have an instant home based business.
- Ordinary people are making money and are producing extraordinary financial results.

I know that when most people think of Ebay they have a picture in their mind of people selling things that they found tucked away and collecting dust in their garage or closet, but over the years Ebay has evolved to be much more than that. It is used by major companies, small business owners and entrepreneurs as a vehicle to hawk their products and services. It is also one of the best testing grounds when trying to evaluate whether or not you have a commercially viable product or service.

I've been an Ebay seller for more than a decade and I have sold a ton of products and services. In fact, I am an Ebay PowerSeller. What is an Ebay PowerSeller? A powerseller is a seller that Ebay distinguishes from the average Joe or Jane that sells on Ebay. A requirement to become a powerseller on Ebay is that you must consistently sell items on a monthly basis and make a certain dollar amount.

In fact, I've become such a prolific seller on Ebay that I have developed some incredible strategies that will enable you to successfully sell your products and services on Ebay. I've written a book entitled "The Secrets Of Making $10,000 On Ebay In 30 Days" that explains in detail the particular strategies that I use.

Open an Ebay Store

One of the great things about Ebay is that you are able to open up a store for your business. This enables you to extend, promote and exposed your brand to a worldwide targeted audience on the Ebay platform. Other advantages of opening a store on Ebay are the following:

- You are able to cross-promote your merchandise.
- There are lower listing fees and longer listing periods.
- You are able to customize and personalize your store.
- When you open an Ebay store you have a unique url that will be picked up by the search engines. You can promote your url online or offline.
- Your Ebay store is open for business 24 hours a day, 7 days a week and 365 days out of the year.
- Customize and personalize your store- Ebay allows the store seller to create custom headers and store front pages using html.
- One of the super benefits of becoming an Ebay store owner is that your store is automatically included in the Ebay store directory, which is promoted to millions of Ebay members.

There are three levels of Ebay stores that you can open up for your business:

Basic- This level is for sellers who are just starting out. Currently there is a monthly charge of $15.95 per month.

Premium- Designed for medium size sellers who want to grow their online business. The subscription fee for the premium store is currently $49.95 per month.

Anchor- An advance store with solutions for high-volume sellers who want maximum Ebay exposure. The subscription fee for the anchor store is currently $299.95 per month.

To open an Ebay store simply go to Ebay's home page and click on the link Ebay stores. Then click on the link "Open a Store" and follow the necessary steps to set up your store.

You don't necessarily have to sell your products or services directly on Ebay to utilize its platform. Here are some of the other alternatives Ebay has to offer:

Classifieds

Ebay classifieds offers users the chance to post ads targeted to potential customers in their area; a great way to reach people in your city and promote your products, services, and business locally.

Display Advertising

Ebay has transformed into more than just an ecommerce platform; it is a vehicle for media as well as an environment where business owners can communicate with their customers. Ebay display advertising is able to target potential customers based on location, demographic, and even their purchase behavior –enabling you to target people who have already bought products similar (or complementary) to your own.

Partnerships

Ebay is also open to direct partnerships, where you can contact them to work together to gain mutual benefits and work together to achieve success. Who wouldn't want to become a partner with one of the biggest companies in the world?

Discussion Groups

Ebay groups allow users to join ongoing discussions with people with common interests. This means that you, as an online marketer, can join groups on topics related to your business to build relationships with potential customers. This is a more social approach to online marketing, but effective nonetheless.

How to Market Your Business Online Using Amazon

Amazon.com is among the top ranking websites both in the US and worldwide. It has earned the trust of web surfers throughout the years and still keeps on doing it by striving towards great customer satisfaction and improving its user's experience.

It is no wonder that more and more people are using it to sell their products –especially since it is an ecommerce platform that has over 300 million credit card users on file. Furthermore, Amazon allows it sellers to set up shop and sell pretty much any type of product they want.

Aside from selling your products directly on their website or becoming an affiliate, Amazon.com also offers several different ways to promote your business which includes the following options:

- **Write reviews.** There are probably a thousand products listed on Amazon that are related to (or complement) your own products. One of the easiest ways to garner attention and be seen as an expert on Amazon.com is by writing a review. What's even better is if you are able to upload a video review of products that you have purchased.

- **Amazon Product PPC ads.** This is another great way to sell your products, without actually selling them on Amazon.com. How? You simply create a product catalog so

Amazon can display it when users search for similar products. However, if a person is interested, they'll click on the advertisement, which leads to a product page on your own website, and they can buy directly from you. You pay Amazon every time your product gets clicked on, and believe me it is a worthwhile investment because you are able to tap into Amazon's traffic which consists mostly of buyers.

- **Display Advertising.** Amazon also offers display advertising. When you utilize display advertising you are able to engage customers with your brand or drive direct response with display ads on Amazon sites, across the web, on mobile and Kindle.

- **AmazonLocal.** This option allows you to connect with potential customers in your area through special deals and offers. Amazon specialists will help you create a promotion, which will be sent to AmazonLocal customers in your area via e-mail. These people can either go to Amazon to find out more about the offer, or go straight to your door to find out more.

  The best part of this option is you don't have to pay to run the promotion! So, how does Amazon make money with this? Quite simply: Amazon processes payments and collects a referral fee in the end –it can't get any easier than that!

How to Market Your Business Online Using Search Engine Marketing

Search engine marketing is basically a form of internet marketing that encompasses the promotion of websites by increasing their visibility in the organic search engine results through optimization (both on-page and off-page) as well as through paid advertising like pay per click.

We have already covered search engine marketing as it relates to pay per click advertising, now we are going to go over search engine marketing as it relates to improving a website's organic search results through SEO. So what exactly is SEO? SEO is an acronym for search engine optimization. It is the process and science of making sure that a website remains relevant to the search engines by ranking high for its main keywords and keyword phrases. This process includes on-page optimization and off-page optimization.

On-page optimization entails working directly on the elements on your website to get it to rank high in the organic search engines and off page optimization entails everything that you do off your website to get it to rank high on the search engines. When I say "organic" search engines, I'm talking about the search engine results that come up that are not paid for via paid advertising. They are essentially free and natural and are referred to as "organic".

On-page optimization factors include some of the following:

Keyword Research, Analysis and Implementation – You must do keyword research for your website. Keyword research is basically determining the best possible keywords that apply to your site. These are the main keywords that you want to rank high for when a search engine query is performed. Once you have determined your main keywords, you must analyze your website to see if there is enough keyword density and keyword prominence to get you ranked for those particular keywords in the search engines.

Keyword density is the percentage of times a keyword or keyword phrase appears on a web page compared to the total number of words on the page. Keyword prominence refers to the prominent placement of keywords or keyword phrases within a web page. Prominent placement may be in the page header, meta tags, opening paragraph, or at the start of a sentence.

Once your analysis is done, you must implement the necessary changes to your site so that you have the chance to rank high in the search engines as well as attract targeted visitors to your site.

Meta Tags - Meta tags are HTML codes that are inserted into the header on a web page, after the title tag. Meta tags are not viewable by your website's visitors. Meta Tags in the past use to be at the top of the list as the main ranking variable that search engines used to determine where a site will rank, but that is no longer the case.

Heading or H Tags - Headings are pieces of html code that allow you to make certain words stand out on a web page. The most important heading tags to search engines are H1 tags. The H1 tag is the highest level tag that guides search engine crawlers to the most relevant words on a web page. There are six types of header tags that range from H1 to H6.

As mentioned previously off–page optimization is everything that you do off your website to get it to rank high. Off-page optimization primarily involves getting backlinks to your website. Backlinks also referred to as inbound links are basically links that are directed towards your website.

The number of quality backlinks that your site has is an indication to the search engines of the popularity or importance of your website and is used to determine where your site will rank. Backlinks are also hugely important because they bring traffic to your website.

Here are some of the ways that you can get quality backlinks to your website:

Article writing and submission – I covered the topic of article writing and submission earlier as an online marketing tactic that you can use to attract your targeted audience, however, it can also be used as way to get much needed quality backlinks to your site.

Social Bookmarking – Social bookmarking allows people to share bookmarks to websites that they think would be of interest to others. In short, social bookmarking websites are sites that categorize and store 'bookmarks' just like you would add a site to your Favorites. Only in this case they are accessible to anyone on the internet. Millions of people visit social bookmarking sites every day looking for recommended sites. These sites get millions of visitors and are great for generating targeted traffic to your website as well as creating automatic backlinks that will enable your website to increase its ranking in the search engines.

Please be aware that I only briefly described how you can use SEO to catapult your rankings in the major search engines. A much more detailed explanation of SEO and how to effectively utilize it can be found in my book entitled Search Engine Domination: "The Ultimate Secrets To Increasing Your Website's Visibility And Making A Ton Of Cash".

In addition, I am also an SEO expert and owner of a SEO company called Get SEO Backlinks (http://www.getseobacklinks.com) that can assist you in your quest to get your business website to rank high in the major search engines for its main keywords.

At Get SEO Backlinks, we have a proven track record and we not only offer you a superior SEO plan for your business, but we also give you a superior backlinking copywriting strategy that will enable your website to convert visitors into customers.

Here is a brief run-down of the services that we have to offer:

Keyword Analysis

We will do a detailed keyword analysis of your website and also give you a ranking report to show you exactly where you currently stand on the 3 major search engines top 100 positions for your website's existing keywords.

On Page Optimization

We will point out the various ways in which you can better optimize your website so that it is search engine friendly.

Competitor Analysis

Competitor Analysis is the process of extensively researching your competitors. We would first make a list of your main competitors and analyze their sites using our state of the art software to decipher and decode the various techniques used by them.

We will also determine how many backlinks they have and where they are receiving those backlinks from. This will enable us to put together a comprehensive link building strategy for you.

SEO Copywriting Assistance

We analyze your website's copy and its SEO elements and make the necessary recommendations to you to ensure that your website is in the position to convert visitors into sales.

Off Page Optimization (Link Building)

After determining the amount of backlinks your first page competitors have, we will begin to gradually build quality premium backlinks to your website. Not only do we build quality premium backlinks to your site, but we will get those backlinks indexed in the search engines with our proprietary link indexing system. Why is the indexing of your backlinks important to your website's well-being? Because search engines don't count backlinks they can't see.

How to Market Your Business Online using Online Business Directories

There are many online business directories that are available and you should strongly consider having your business listed in them. The great thing about being listed in an online business directory is it is another way that your targeted audience can find you online.

For example, let's say you owned a carpet cleaning business in Miami and you listed your business in an online directory. When a potential customer who is also located in Miami is looking for a business in their local area that specializes in cleaning carpets they usually go to a search engine like Google and enter in the following keyword in their search query "Carpet cleaning service Miami".

If you have a website for your carpet cleaning business and it is optimized properly, chances are that it might come up in the search results and that person might find you. However, if they can't find your website maybe the business directory that your carpet cleaning service is listed in shows up in the search results. If this were the case, they can then click on the link that leads to that directory explore it, and perhaps discover your business.

This is not a far-fetched scenario, because most business directories are highly optimized so they rank high in the search engines. Also, they are well promoted by their owners which is another added benefit. Some online business directories just focus only on one particular niche. For example, there are directories that are solely dedicated to promoting accountants. There are ones that list only lawyers etc.

To find the online business directories that are suited to your particular business, just Google your field of specialty and include the keywords "business directory" and you will have no trouble finding one or several. Most of these types of directories require a fee for you to get listed in them. Conversely, there are also general directories that you can list your business in to get additional exposure.

These are mainly free of charge with some of them requiring that you reciprocally link back to their website. My company Get SEO Backlinks (http://www.getseobacklinks.com) also can do these types of directory submissions for you.

How to Market Your Business Online Using Mobile Apps

As a business owner and entrepreneur you never want to leave money on the table. Am I right? You are far too savvy for that! However, most business owners and entrepreneurs are in fact guilty when it comes to leaving money on the table if they are not utilizing the phenomenon of mobile marketing to get customers for their business.

Mobile marketing should be one of the most important aspects of nearly every business owner's marketing plan, but is all too often overlooked. Why is mobile marketing significant to your business? It's quite obvious. More than 70% of the world's population now has access to a mobile device and that includes your targeted prospects as well as your current customers. So, it is critical for your business to have a mobile marketing plan. Without it, you severely decrease your chances of marketing to a larger audience.

Mobile Technology has shifted behavior

There are 5 billion active mobile subscriptions in the world today. When you take into consideration that there are only 6 billion people in the world, and just a little over 1 billion personal computers, you can see that by not considering mobile users when you put together your marketing plan would be a huge mistake, that's why it is imperative that your business engage in mobile content marketing.

What exactly is mobile content? Mobile content is anything that is read, listened to or viewed on mobile phones. Here are some examples of mobile content:

- RSS feeds
- Apps that give you information (e.g. nearest restaurant, traveling conditions for your area, web stores carrying products you want)
- Apps that help you function more effectively (e.g. organizers, calendars, voice reminders)
- Books on audio
- TV shows
- Books in a reader such as Amazon's Kindle
- Videos formatted for small screen
- Your favorite music
- Instructional MP3 files
- Text messages
- Voice message

Mobile marketing is not only just about presenting your website in a mobile-friendly manner. Of course that is important, but there is much more to mobile marketing than just having an optimized website.

Creating a Mobile APP for Your Business

Apple and Google changed the mobile industry game with the invention of the IPhone and Android technology respectively. Most people who use smartphones are either using IPhones or smartphones that run on the Android technology. Smartphone usage has grown and will continue to grow by leaps and bounds.

In fact, according to Comscore, there are over 100 million smart phone users in the United States alone. The proliferation of smart phones throughout the world has given birth to an entirely new and booming industry called mobile applications. Mobile applications or mobile apps are basically software programs for mobile phones that you can download and access directly on a smartphone. Mobile apps are mostly free and they allow you to play games, get turn-by-turn directions, access news, books, weather, music, videos and host of other things.

The mobile app industry is growing at a phenomenal rate. In 2011, the revenue of the mobile app industry was $8.5 billion and that number is expected to increase to $46 billion by the year of 2016. As smartphone users become more use to mobile advertisements and in store app purchases, businesses are not only recognizing new marketing opportunities via mobile apps, but are capitalizing profit wise by creating their own applications.

So before you go rush off and start creating apps for your business, first start by asking yourself the following questions.

What is the best app for my customers?

What do they want?

Also keep in mind that your mobile app doesn't have to be the most brilliant app in the world. It just has to be:

- Something that your customers need
- Something that they can rely on
- Something that's interesting and appealing

There are sites that allow you to create apps without knowing a single word of code. Here are two of those sites.

1) GENWI (http://genwi.com/)
2) http://www.MyAppBuilder.com

Self building app sites are wonderful for their simplicity and if you don't mind using basic templates. However, for more complex app building you should definitely outsource your app building tasks. Here are a few sites where you can find app developers:

http://www.iphonefreelancer.com/

http://www.odesk.com

http://www.freelancer.com

Here are 3 essential tips that will help you with your app outsourcing experience:

1) Simpler is better. The more complex your mobile app is, the longer the project will take. The longer your project takes, the higher the price. (You should plan in your budget to spend anywhere from $500 upwards in order to end up with a professional, glitch-free app.)

2) Look for developers that ask for a deposit or retainer – Whatever you do not pay the full amount up front. When you do that you basically have no protection! You can even structure your entire payment based on milestone achievements.

3) Make sure that you get signed a non-disclosure agreement (NDA) and a non-competitor agreement (NCA). This guarantees that your app developer won't let your competition know about the details of the app that they are

creating for you and they won't be able to launch a competing version of the same app.

Making Money with Your Apps

There are several different ways that you can make money with your apps. You can sell your apps, you can offer in-app purchases, or you can use AdMob by Google to monetize your apps. The concept of making money by using AdMob is quite simple. Ads from Google advertisers are displayed in your app and users click on the ads that they like. When they click on the ads that they like, you make money.

To maximize your marketing opportunities and to expand your brand to a wider audience it is essential that you utilize mobile technology to the fullest by exploiting mobile content marketing and the creation of apps.

How to Market Your Business Online Using CraigsList

I know I have covered online classified advertising already, but I feel that it is important for me to give Craigslist its own special attention because it is one of the most known and recognized sites in the world. What in the heck is Craigslist? Craigslist is a centralized network of online communities, featuring free online classified advertisements and was founded by Craig Newmark in 1996.

Craigslist hosts over 300 communities and receives over 15 million visitors monthly. Obviously Craigslist should be a part of your business's marketing arsenal, because it's a convenient way to reach your targeted audience, plus it's free (unless it relates to a job posting) which makes it even more appealing. In addition, if you wanted to market your business locally Craigslist is the ideal place to do it.

In fact, you can easily promote your product or service by posting your ads in the appropriate section. For example, if you were promoting a service, you can place your ad in the service section of Craigslist. The service section is even more targeted because it is broken down into the following categories below and I'm quite sure you can find one that pertains to your business.

Craigslist Services Section

1) Beauty
2) Creative
3) Computer
4) Cycle
5) Event
6) Financial
7) Legal
8) Lessons
9) Marine
10) Pet
11) Automotive
12) Farm+Garden
13) Household
14) Labor/Move
15) Skill'd Trade
16) Real Estate
17) Sm Biz Ads
18) Therapeutic
19) Travel/Vacation
20) Writing/Editing/Translation

Craigslist also has an extensive category selection that you can choose from when listing your products in the "For Sale" section. In the "For Sale" section, you are allowed to sell both new and used items.

To further reach your targeted audience, Craigslist has a discussion forum in every niche imaginable that you can participate in. The discussion forum is a great place where you can provide insightful information, and provide people with accurate responses to questions that they may have raised.

However, I must note that when taking part in forum discussions, you avoid making your postings in such a way that people will look at them and think that they are spam. If they feel that your posts are spam they will "flag" you and your posts will get deleted by Craigslist and if you are a repeated offender they may remove you from being a subscriber to their service.

Another advantage of posting ads on Craigslist is you are allowed to post in a different state and city other than your own. However, you are only allowed to choose just ONE local craigslist site for which your ad is most relevant.

Here are some useful tips to help you get started on Craigslist:

Open an account – You don't have to register an account to start posting your ads but having one sure makes it easier for you. By having an account you can post, edit and delete your ads. You will also be able to repost much easier.

Write an effective ad- In order to get the response you want, you need to write an effective ad. Here are some tips that will enable you to do so:

Make sure you write a great title – a great title will entice the reader to click on your ad. So try to be descriptive as possible and try to include some of the benefits in the title.

Make sure you write a great description – just like the title of the ad, you want to make sure that you write a great and detailed description. Tell readers of your ad exactly what they are going to get and don't forget to put the price.

Don't forget to include a "call to action" – What is the purpose of your ad? What do you want it to accomplish? Do you want your prospects to call you, email you or visit your website? In order for them to do exactly what you want, you have to include the right "call to action".

Make sure you repost your ad -When other Craigslist ads are posted yours will naturally drop, so make sure to repost your ads. You are allowed to repost your Craigslist ad after 48 hours has lapsed.

How to Market Your Business Online Using Banner Ads

Banner advertising can be a great way to market your business online because they can help you increase traffic to your website, generate sales and increase brand awareness. So, what exactly is banner advertising? A "web banner" or "banner ad" is a form of advertising on the internet that entails embedding an advertisement into a web page. The whole purpose of a banner ad is to drive traffic back to your website from the site that you are advertising on. This is accomplished by your banner being linked back to your website via the insertion of your URL in the html code of the banner.

A banner ad is a rectangular, square image or button image in shape and it appears alongside of the content of the website that you wish to advertise on. They are usually tall and thin (appearing at the side of the page), or short and wide (appearing at the top or bottom of the page). Banner ads can contain animation, audio or video to enhance or maximize their presence.

Banner ads come in various sizes and are measured by pixels. The most popular size is usually 468X60 however, there are other sizes that you can consider. Here are the standard sizes when it comes to banner ads.

468 x 60 - Full Banner

728 x 90 – Leader board

336 x 280 - Square

300 x 250 - Square

250 x 250 - Square

160 x 600 -Skyscraper

120 x 600 - Skyscraper

120 x 240 -Small Skyscraper

240 x 400 - Fat Skyscraper

234 x 60 - Half Banner

180 x 150 - Rectangle

125 x 125 - Square Button

120 x 90 - Button

120 x 60 - Button

88 x 31 – Button

When creating banner ads to promote and advertise your business, you should make sure that they are visually appealing and contain text or audio that draws interest to them. Remember the whole point of banner advertising is to get the viewers to click on the banner so that they can be directed back to your website where you can further sell them on your products or services. So as a general rule your banner ad should be:

- **Informative** – You can include your core message or unique selling position (USP)
- **Simple** – Don't design anything crazy or overboard that will distract from your message and dampen interest.
- **Eye catching** – As mentioned previously you can use animation, sound or video to enhance and maximize your banner's presence.
- **Targeted** – Make sure your that your banner advertising campaign is targeted to the audience that you are trying to attract.

There are several different ways that you can find websites to display your banner ads:

Contact the website yourself – If you see a website that is relevant and contains your targeted audience, you can simply contact them and inquire about banner advertising.

Banner exchange programs – Banner exchanges are a way to advertise your banner on other websites. The way that it works is you agree to display a number of banner advertisements on your own website in return for yours being shown. However, the catch is you usually have to display more advertisements on your own site than they will display for you. That ratio is usually 2 to 1.

Advertising agency – An advertising agency can handle all of your banner advertising tasks like placement and negotiation of prices. They will guide you and lend their expertise to the whole banner advertising process.

Banner ad networks – Banner ad networks act as brokers between advertisers and publishers. They are similar to banner exchange programs and they handle the responsibility of placing an advertiser's banner ad as well as all tracking related to it. Here are some of those banner advertising networks below to get you started:

> http://web.blogads.com
>
> http://mediatraffic.com
>
> http://casalemedia.com
>
> http://tribalfusion.com
>
> http://kontera.com
>
> http://bidvertiser.com
>
> http://chitika.com
>
> http://cpxinteractive.com
>
> http://clicksor.com
>
> http://advertising.com
>
> http://valueclickmedia.com
>
> http://www.specificmedia.com
>
> http://adbrite.com
>
> http://buysellads.com
>
> http://www.burstmedia.com
>
> http://www.adperium.com/directads
>
> http://adonnetwork.com

These are some of the pricing methods that publishers use to charge advertisers for banners ads:

Cost per click (CPC) – You are charged per click when anytime someone clicks on your banner.

Cost per view (CPV) – As an advertiser you pay for each unique user view of your banner ad.

Cost per thousand (CPM, CPI) – You are charged per thousand impressions.

How to Market Your Business Online Using QR Codes

Before we get into how you can use QR codes to market your business online let me first tell you what they are and their history. QR stands for quick response and a QR code is similar to but is a much more fancier version of the barcode. In fact, the only difference between the two is that a QR code carries a lot more data than a traditional bar code.

Historically, the QR code was created by a company called Denso which is owned by Toyota and it was invented in order to improve the speed by which they assembled cars in the factory.

Perhaps you have a seen QR codes before? They are those funny looking square designs that contain a multitude of black dots and there is a good chance of you seeing them in magazines, newspapers, on direct mail, and plastered on places of business. These multitude of black dots represent either a 1 or a 0 (zero) in binary code and when combined in a series the dots and spaces make up what the QR code is saying.

A smartphone if it contains an app that is designed especially to decipher QR codes can then scan the code, read it and interpret its contents back to the user. Are you starting to see the possibilities and the power of using QR codes to market your business? The possibilities are indeed endless.

In fact, here are some of the creative ways you can use QR codes.

- **Information tool for your business**. If you are a local business you can put a QR code on your doors that contain information about your business's opening and closing time, its phone number and website address, and information pertaining to the products and services that you offer.

- **On business cards**. Putting your QR code on a business card is presently the most popular way that businesses are using QR codes.

- **In print ads**. If you're running a coupon special offer you can have a QR code link to download the coupon that has to be presented at your place of business.

- **Rewards Program.** You can use QR codes in your rewards program that you offer to your customers. You can set up a QR code that has to be scanned whenever someone purchases a product or service. After x amount of scans, they get a coupon or gift certificate that they can instantly redeem.

You can create your own QR codes by using free services like Kaywa and Delivr, although Delivr has much more advanced features like being able to edit the URL you are pointing your QR code to. This allows you to reuse the same QR code over and over again.

Message to Market Match

Whether you are engaged in marketing online or offline you must make sure that your message matches your market and you are marketing through the right medium, because if you don't your marketing will be rendered ineffective, wasting your precious time, money and energy. To give you an idea what I mean by a "message to market match" here's an example.

If you owned a car dealership that specialized in selling only new high-end luxurious Mercedes Benzes, BMWs, and Lexuses it would be foolish for you to advertise the cars that you have for sale in a magazine called "Used Cars Enthusiasts", because your product and core message "new high-end luxurious cars for sale" would not match that particular audience who reads or subscribes to the "Used Car Enthusiasts" magazine. Obviously that audience's primary interests are used cars, so instead of having a match there is a mismatch with both the message and the medium which in this case is the "Used Car Enthusiasts" publication.

On the other hand if you advertised in a magazine called "High End Car Buyers" who reader's and subscriber's demographics and psychographics consisted of people who previously bought and are interested in the latest high end cars, then your message will assuredly match the market or target audience you ideally want to reach because it is being conveyed through the right medium.

When deciding where you should promote and advertise your products and services, and to make sure that you are choosing the right path, here are some of the questions that you need to ask yourself.

1) Is it the right medium?
2) Does it have the audience that I'm trying to target?
3) Does my core marketing message match the audience?
4) What are the demographics?
5) What are the psychographics?
6) How many people can I potentially reach?

In addition, you should also research how other advertisers have fared in the past with the magazine, newspaper, newsletter etc. that you wish to market your products or services in. The way that you would do this is by looking at the current issue and record the list of advertisers that are in your field. Then you would look at the previous or back issues to see if the same advertisers are present. If you see that they have been advertising consistently this is a good indication that they are receiving positive results from their ads. Needless to say, if they weren't they would of logically stopped advertising.

Tweaking your message

Once your ad runs, monitor the results. If you are not satisfied with the results or you want to improve upon your results, you might want to tweak your ad a little or change your message altogether to get a better response. For example, I placed the following ad below for my real estate marketing home study course "The Real Estate Investors Guide To Finding Motivated Sellers" in a publication that catered exclusively to real estate investors and it yielded so-so results.

Find Motivated Sellers
Comprehensive Home Study Course
shows you step by step how to attract
and find motivated sellers. Visit:
http://www.findingthemotivatedsellers.com

When I tweaked that ad and changed the message to the following it exploded my sales.

Find Motivated Sellers
Ready to use marketing system will enable
you to find and attract motivated sellers
by the boatload even if they're hiding under a rock.
Visit: http://www.findingthemotivatedsellers.com

This ad's success was based on the reframing of the core message. Instead of positioning it as just a home study course I repositioned it as a "ready to use" marketing system. The tweaked ad is much more powerful than the original ad because the words that I used were more vivid and descriptive. Simply put, they contained magic words or phrases that sell. The lesson here is: don't be afraid to test and tweak your ad copy to achieve optimum results.

You have to be a Disciplined Marketer

Marketing is not something that you should ever take a break from. It should be something that you should be doing all of the time unless the marketplace tells you they no longer need your products or services. In that case, you will simply go out of business. Since marketing is something that you need to be doing all of the time, it is essential that you become a disciplined marketer.

To become disciplined at marketing you have to establish a daily routine or ritual. To illustrate my point, let me give you a sports analogy. Lebron James is arguably the best basketball player on the planet. He has reached that point and continues to sustain it because of his daily routine which involves hours of practice working on and refining his skills and staying in optimum physical shape. This disciplined approach to his profession results in him having tremendous and consistent success on the basketball court.

As a marketer, you have to have a similar mindset. What is a mindset? A mindset is universally defined as a habitual or characteristic mental attitude that determines how you will interpret and respond to situations. A situation could involve a specific task or goal. For example, in order for you to be one of the dominant businesses in your niche or the dominant business in your niche you have to have a strong mindset when it comes to marketing, innovation, and execution. You have to be willing to do the things that others in your niche are not willing to do especially in regards to marketing.

For instance, you may have a super ambitious goal of being the preeminent player in your niche when it comes to video marketing. This may require you to create and upload let's say 730 videos consisting of various subject matter relating to your industry or your products or services. To accomplish a feat like this, you first have to have the mindset or belief that you can actually do it. Once that belief is established you have to be disciplined as a marketer to get it done and that includes devising a strategy and a plan to accomplish this goal in a specific time frame.

Let's say that your time frame is one year. How many videos would you be able to create and upload to YouTube every day to reach your goal in a year? Let's say hypothetically that it's 4 videos per day. You would reach your goal in six months which is really ambitious. However, 4 videos per day might not be feasible for you so you decide on two videos a day. By creating and uploading 2 videos per day on YouTube it would take you exactly 1 year to accomplish your goal of being the preeminent player in your niche or industry when it comes to video marketing.

The point that I am trying to get across here is simply this: You have to be a disciplined marketer and have a strong mindset to reach and accomplish your marketing goals.

Strategy and Execution are the Keys to Your Success

In conclusion, I have given you many online and offline marketing tactics that can propel your business into the next stratosphere in terms of visibility and profitability, but you must realize that marketing tactics are just part of the success equation. The other parts of the success equation also include your overall strategy for your business and ultimately your execution of that strategy.

So in regards to the overall strategy of your business, you must make sure that it is well defined, because if it's not you will find yourself all over the place moving in different directions and even in an opposite direction than what you intended. Once you have a well defined strategy, you have to execute, plain and simple.

What is execution? Execution is actually putting your marketing plan into action. Execution is critical to your success and without a carefully planned approach to your execution your strategic goals can't be accomplished. It's the equivalent of someone making a new year's resolution to lose weight, but not following through and doing the things necessary to accomplishing that goal like exercising more, dieting etc. So remember to always execute, because if you don't your goals and strategy are nothing more than a pipe dream.

I hope you have enjoyed reading this book and more importantly I hope that you've picked up a great deal of online and offline marketing ideas that you can immediately implement in your business. If you need further assistance in formulating and executing a marketing plan for your business I offer consulting. Here is my contact information:

Omar Johnson
Make Profits Easy LLC
497 West Side Avenue
Suite 134
Jersey City, New Jersey 07304
Telephone # (917) 406-3549
Email: profitsdaily123@aol.com

Good luck and much success,

Omar Johnson

Other Books by Author

Search Engine Domination: "The Ultimate Secrets To Increasing Your Website's Visibility And Making a Ton of Cash"

How To Sell Any Product Online: "Secrets of The Killer Sales Letter"

How To Make Money Online: "The Savvy Entrepreneur's Guide to Financial Freedom"

How To Create A Profitable Ezine From Scratch

The Secrets of Finding The Perfect Ghostwriter For Your Book

How To Overcome Your Self-Limiting Beliefs & Achieve Anything You Want

Creative Real Estate Investing Strategies and Tips

How To Make A Fortune Using The Public Domain

The Complete Guide To Investing In Gold And Silver: Surviving The Great Economic Depression

How To Promote Market And Sell Your Kindle Book

How To Start An Online Business With Less Than $200

The Secrets of Making $10,000 On Ebay In 30 Days

The Creative Real Estate Marketing Equation: Motivated Sellers + Motivated Buyers = $

www.ingramcontent.com/pod-product-compliance
Lightning Source LLC
Chambersburg PA
CBHW061510180526
45171CB00001B/115